Hello!

I'm so glad that this journal found you.

Before you begin, please read the following. However, brace yourself for some word vomit. I know, it's long... But don't worry, it's not useless. The intention of the following is to set the tone for using this journal.

Backstory :

Data collection is ubiquitous in today's society as it is a stepping stone for all kinds of advancements. Collecting data is a systematic approach to gathering and analyzing information to provide an individual with an aerial view of the evidence of interest. The goal is to enable the seeker(s) to organize information, answer questions, make predictions, make informed decisions, etc. in the efforts to increase profit, efficiency and productivity.

"Okay, but this is a journal, so why should I care about data collection? This isn't a math class. "

Well, I'm thrilled that you asked.

We go about our daily lives with such robotic automation — each day blurring into the next. To keep up with demands and deadlines, we make conscious and subconscious sacrifices. Sadly, those sacrifices usually concern ourselves. When was the last time you made yourself a priority?

The Maximalist bullet journal was created with the intention of giving you a space to evaluate and keep track of all the things in YOUR own life, all while engaging in a creative outlet. In the following year, you will be able to capture a range of information that you may not prioritize every day like you should, so that you may recognize the steps you must take to improve yourself mentally, physically, emotionally, and spiritually.

This bullet journal is not only a data tracker — it is also a colouring book, each page filled with artwork that will come to life thanks to your artistry. So crack your knuckles, Picasso, and get lost in your art.

Overall, this bullet journal will help generate mindfulness, quietness and well-being, while reducing stress and anxiety so that you may live life as the most authentic version of yourself.

It's time to nurture yourself.

With love and light,

Michelle

MONTHLY
PAGES

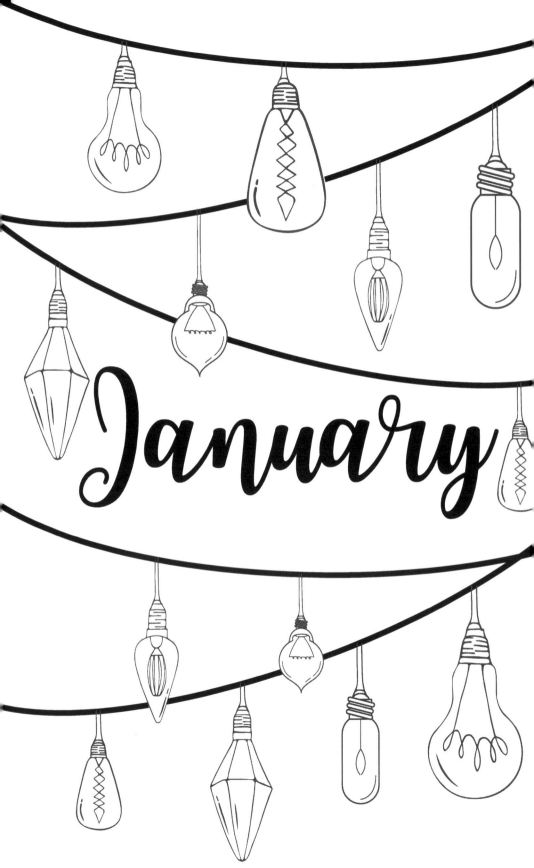

WHERE THERE IS LIGHT, THERE IS ALSO DARKNESS. EMBRACE ALL THE PARTS OF YOURSELF

JANUARY

january

2022

SUNDAY	MONDAY	TUESDAY	WEDNESDAY
2	3	4	5
9	10	11	12
16	17	18	19
23	24	25	26
30	31		

SATURDAY

THURSDAY	FRIDAY	
		1
6	7	8
13	14	15
20	21	22
27	28	29

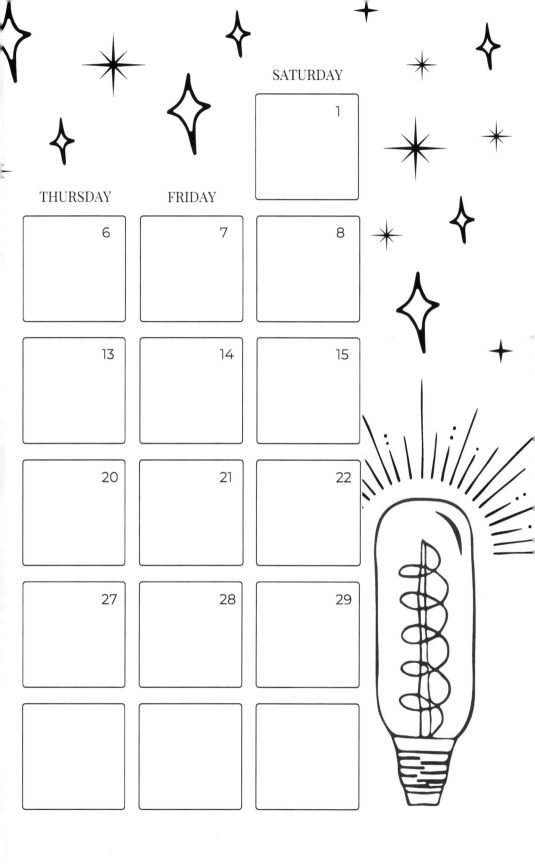

Highlight of the day

1 ---
2 ---
3 ---
4 ---
5 ---
6 ---
7 ---
8 ---
9 ---
10 --
11 --
12 --
13 --
14 --
15 --
16 --
17 --
18 --
19 --
20 --
21 --
22 --
23 --
24 --
25 --
26 --
27 --
28 --
29 --
30 --
31 --

AFFIRMATION
board

SEEK THE
light

Monthly Sleep Tracker

	PM					AM												PM						
1	**7**	**8**	**9**	**10**	**11**	12	1	2	3	4	5	6	7	8	9	10	11	**12**	**1**	2	3	4	5	6
2	**7**	**8**	**9**	**10**	**11**	12	1	2	3	4	5	6	7	8	9	10	11	**12**	**1**	2	3	4	5	6
3	**7**	**8**	**9**	**10**	**11**	12	1	2	3	4	5	6	7	8	9	10	11	**12**	**1**	2	3	4	5	6
4	**7**	**8**	**9**	**10**	**11**	12	1	2	3	4	5	6	7	8	9	10	11	**12**	**1**	2	3	4	5	6
5	**7**	**8**	**9**	**10**	**11**	12	1	2	3	4	5	6	7	8	9	10	11	**12**	**1**	2	3	4	5	6
6	**7**	**8**	**9**	**10**	**11**	12	1	2	3	4	5	6	7	8	9	10	11	**12**	**1**	2	3	4	5	6
7	**7**	**8**	**9**	**10**	**11**	12	1	2	3	4	5	6	7	8	9	10	11	**12**	**1**	2	3	4	5	6
8	**7**	**8**	**9**	**10**	**11**	12	1	2	3	4	5	6	7	8	9	10	11	**12**	**1**	2	3	4	5	6
9	**7**	**8**	**9**	**10**	**11**	12	1	2	3	4	5	6	7	8	9	10	11	**12**	**1**	2	3	4	5	6
10	**7**	**8**	**9**	**10**	**11**	12	1	2	3	4	5	6	7	8	9	10	11	**12**	**1**	2	3	4	5	6
11	**7**	**8**	**9**	**10**	**11**	12	1	2	3	4	5	6	7	8	9	10	11	**12**	**1**	2	3	4	5	6
12	**7**	**8**	**9**	**10**	**11**	12	1	2	3	4	5	6	7	8	9	10	11	**12**	**1**	2	3	4	5	6
13	**7**	**8**	**9**	**10**	**11**	12	1	2	3	4	5	6	7	8	9	10	11	**12**	**1**	2	3	4	5	6
14	**7**	**8**	**9**	**10**	**11**	12	1	2	3	4	5	6	7	8	9	10	11	**12**	**1**	2	3	4	5	6
15	**7**	**8**	**9**	**10**	**11**	12	1	2	3	4	5	6	7	8	9	10	11	**12**	**1**	2	3	4	5	6
16	**7**	**8**	**9**	**10**	**11**	12	1	2	3	4	5	6	7	8	9	10	11	**12**	**1**	2	3	4	5	6
17	**7**	**8**	**9**	**10**	**11**	12	1	2	3	4	5	6	7	8	9	10	11	**12**	**1**	2	3	4	5	6
18	**7**	**8**	**9**	**10**	**11**	12	1	2	3	4	5	6	7	8	9	10	11	**12**	**1**	2	3	4	5	6
19	**7**	**8**	**9**	**10**	**11**	12	1	2	3	4	5	6	7	8	9	10	11	**12**	**1**	2	3	4	5	6
20	**7**	**8**	**9**	**10**	**11**	12	1	2	3	4	5	6	7	8	9	10	11	**12**	**1**	2	3	4	5	6
21	**7**	**8**	**9**	**10**	**11**	12	1	2	3	4	5	6	7	8	9	10	11	**12**	**1**	2	3	4	5	6
22	**7**	**8**	**9**	**10**	**11**	12	1	2	3	4	5	6	7	8	9	10	11	**12**	**1**	2	3	4	5	6
23	**7**	**8**	**9**	**10**	**11**	12	1	2	3	4	5	6	7	8	9	10	11	**12**	**1**	2	3	4	5	6
24	**7**	**8**	**9**	**10**	**11**	12	1	2	3	4	5	6	7	8	9	10	11	**12**	**1**	2	3	4	5	6
25	**7**	**8**	**9**	**10**	**11**	12	1	2	3	4	5	6	7	8	9	10	11	**12**	**1**	2	3	4	5	6
26	**7**	**8**	**9**	**10**	**11**	12	1	2	3	4	5	6	7	8	9	10	11	**12**	**1**	2	3	4	5	6
27	**7**	**8**	**9**	**10**	**11**	12	1	2	3	4	5	6	7	8	9	10	11	**12**	**1**	2	3	4	5	6
28	**7**	**8**	**9**	**10**	**11**	12	1	2	3	4	5	6	7	8	9	10	11	**12**	**1**	2	3	4	5	6
29	**7**	**8**	**9**	**10**	**11**	12	1	2	3	4	5	6	7	8	9	10	11	**12**	**1**	2	3	4	5	6
30	**7**	**8**	**9**	**10**	**11**	12	1	2	3	4	5	6	7	8	9	10	11	**12**	**1**	2	3	4	5	6
31	**7**	**8**	**9**	**10**	**11**	12	1	2	3	4	5	6	7	8	9	10	11	**12**	**1**	2	3	4	5	6

THINGS TO
remember

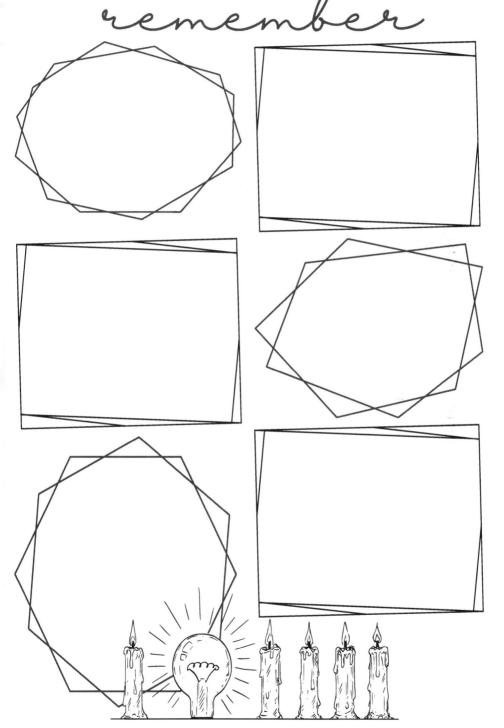

Mood Tracker

Happy   Sad   Grumpy   Energetic

Calm   Anxious   Angry

Normal   Sick   Tired

SELF-CARE
routine

Body

Mind

Soul

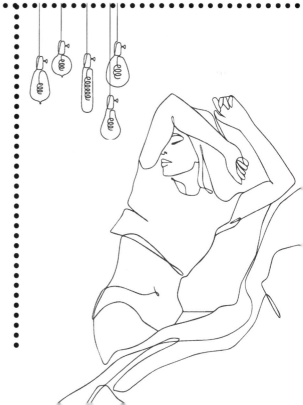

Water Log

COLOUR KEY

 :

 :

 :

 :

1
2
3
4
5
6
7
8
9
10
11
12
13
14
15
16
17
18
19
20
21
22
23
24
25
26
27
28
29
30
31

PLAYLIST

january

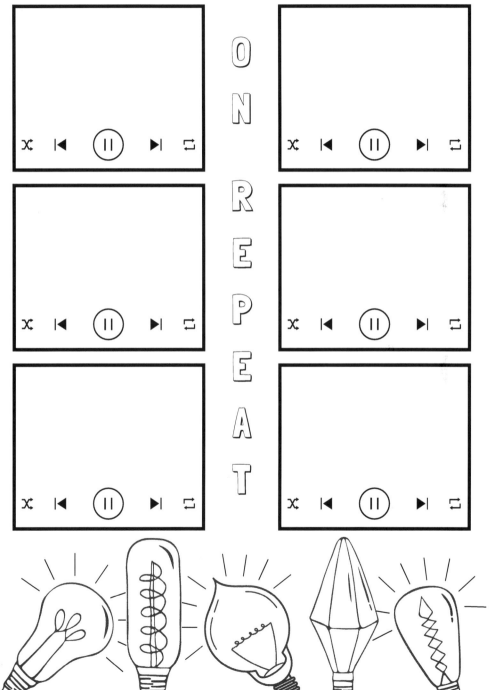

ON REPEAT

Habit Tracker

1 2 3 4 5 6 7
8 9 10 11 12 13 14
15 16 17 18 19 20 21
22 23 24 25 26 27 28
29 30 31

1
2 3
4 5 6
7 8 9 10
11 12 13 14 15 16
17 18 19 20 21 22 23
24 25 26 27 28 29 30 31

1 2 3 4 5 6 7 8 9 10 11 12 13 14 15
16 17 18 19 20 21 22 23 24 25 26 27 28 29 30
31

1 2 3 4 5 6 7
8 9 10 11 12 13 14
15 16 17 18 19 20 21
22 23 24 25 26 27 28
29 30 31

TO-DO LIST

january

NO.	TO DO	Y / N

NOTES

Gratitude Log

1	
2	
3	
4	
5	
6	
7	
8	
9	
10	
11	
12	
13	
14	
15	
16	
17	
18	
19	
20	
21	
22	
23	
24	
25	
26	
27	
28	
29	
30	
31	

VISION
board

MY NOTES

MY DOODLES

February

SET YOUR INTENTIONS AND WATCH THEM BLOSSOM

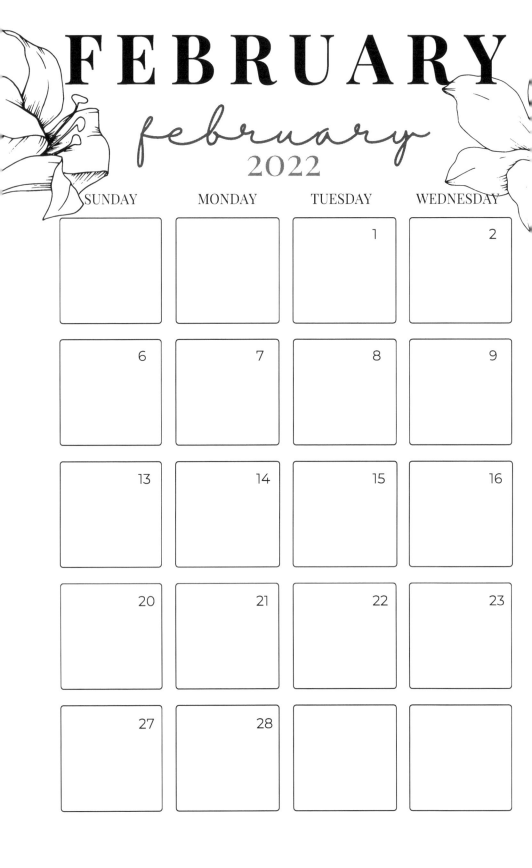

FEBRUARY

february
2022

SUNDAY	MONDAY	TUESDAY	WEDNESDAY
		1	2
6	7	8	9
13	14	15	16
20	21	22	23
27	28		

THURSDAY	FRIDAY	SATURDAY
3	4	5
10	11	12
17	18	19
24	25	26

Highlight of the day

1 --
2 --
3 --
4 --
5 --
6 --
7 --
8 --
9 --
10 ---
11 ---
12 ---
13 ---
14 ---
15 ---
16 ---
17 ---
18 ---
19 ---
20 ---
21 ---
22 ---
23 ---
24 ---
25 ---
26 ---
27 ---
28 ---

AFFIRMATION
board

Monthly Sleep Tracker

	PM					AM															PM						
1	7	8	9	10	11	12	1	2	3	4	5	6	7	8	9	10	11	12	1	2	3	4	5	6
2	7	8	9	10	11	12	1	2	3	4	5	6	7	8	9	10	11	12	1	2	3	4	5	6
3	7	8	9	10	11	12	1	2	3	4	5	6	7	8	9	10	11	12	1	2	3	4	5	6
4	7	8	9	10	11	12	1	2	3	4	5	6	7	8	9	10	11	12	1	2	3	4	5	6
5	7	8	9	10	11	12	1	2	3	4	5	6	7	8	9	10	11	12	1	2	3	4	5	6
6	7	8	9	10	11	12	1	2	3	4	5	6	7	8	9	10	11	12	1	2	3	4	5	6
7	7	8	9	10	11	12	1	2	3	4	5	6	7	8	9	10	11	12	1	2	3	4	5	6
8	7	8	9	10	11	12	1	2	3	4	5	6	7	8	9	10	11	12	1	2	3	4	5	6
9	7	8	9	10	11	12	1	2	3	4	5	6	7	8	9	10	11	12	1	2	3	4	5	6
10	7	8	9	10	11	12	1	2	3	4	5	6	7	8	9	10	11	12	1	2	3	4	5	6
11	7	8	9	10	11	12	1	2	3	4	5	6	7	8	9	10	11	12	1	2	3	4	5	6
12	7	8	9	10	11	12	1	2	3	4	5	6	7	8	9	10	11	12	1	2	3	4	5	6
13	7	8	9	10	11	12	1	2	3	4	5	6	7	8	9	10	11	12	1	2	3	4	5	6
14	7	8	9	10	11	12	1	2	3	4	5	6	7	8	9	10	11	12	1	2	3	4	5	6
15	7	8	9	10	11	12	1	2	3	4	5	6	7	8	9	10	11	12	1	2	3	4	5	6
16	7	8	9	10	11	12	1	2	3	4	5	6	7	8	9	10	11	12	1	2	3	4	5	6
17	7	8	9	10	11	12	1	2	3	4	5	6	7	8	9	10	11	12	1	2	3	4	5	6
18	7	8	9	10	11	12	1	2	3	4	5	6	7	8	9	10	11	12	1	2	3	4	5	6
19	7	8	9	10	11	12	1	2	3	4	5	6	7	8	9	10	11	12	1	2	3	4	5	6
20	7	8	9	10	11	12	1	2	3	4	5	6	7	8	9	10	11	12	1	2	3	4	5	6
21	7	8	9	10	11	12	1	2	3	4	5	6	7	8	9	10	11	12	1	2	3	4	5	6
22	7	8	9	10	11	12	1	2	3	4	5	6	7	8	9	10	11	12	1	2	3	4	5	6
23	7	8	9	10	11	12	1	2	3	4	5	6	7	8	9	10	11	12	1	2	3	4	5	6
24	7	8	9	10	11	12	1	2	3	4	5	6	7	8	9	10	11	12	1	2	3	4	5	6
25	7	8	9	10	11	12	1	2	3	4	5	6	7	8	9	10	11	12	1	2	3	4	5	6
26	7	8	9	10	11	12	1	2	3	4	5	6	7	8	9	10	11	12	1	2	3	4	5	6
27	7	8	9	10	11	12	1	2	3	4	5	6	7	8	9	10	11	12	1	2	3	4	5	6
28	7	8	9	10	11	12	1	2	3	4	5	6	7	8	9	10	11	12	1	2	3	4	5	6

THINGS TO
remember

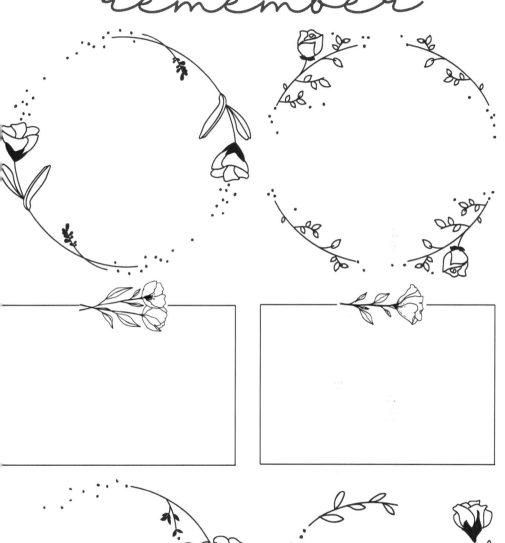

Mood Tracker

1 2 3 4 5 6 7 8 9 10 11 12 13 14 15 16 17 18 19 20 21 22 23 24 25 26 27 28

○ Happy   ○ Sad   ○ Grumpy   ○ Energetic

○ Calm   ○ Anxious   ○ Angry   ○

○ Normal   ○ Sick   ○ Tired   ○

SELF-CARE
routine

Body

Mind

Soul

NOTE TO SELF:

more self love

Water Log

COLOUR KEY

 :

 :

 :

 :

1
2
3
4
5
6
7
8
9
10
11
12
13
14
15
16
17
18
19
20
21
22
23
24
25
26
27
28

PLAYLIST
february

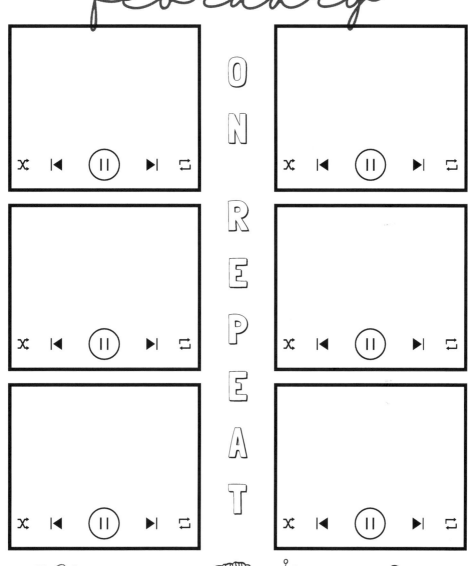

O N   R E P E A T

Habit Tracker

1 2 3 4 5 6 7 8 9 10 11 12
13 14 15 16 17 18 19 20 21 22 23 24
25 26 27 28

1 2 3 4
5 6 7 8
9 10 11 12
13 14 15 16
17 18 19 20
21 22 23 24
25 26 27 28

1 2 3 4 5 6 7
8 9 10 11 12 13 14
15 16 17 18 19 20 21
22 23 24 25 26 27 28

1 2 3 4 5 6 7
8 9 10 11 12 13 14
15 16 17 18 19 20 21
22 23 24 25 26 27 28

TO-DO LIST
february

NO.	TO DO	Y / N

NOTES	

Gratitude Log

1	
2	
3	
4	
5	
6	
7	
8	
9	
10	
11	
12	
13	
14	
15	
16	
17	
18	
19	
20	
21	
22	
23	
24	
25	
26	
27	
28	

VISION
board

MY NOTES

MY DOODLES

IT'S MY TIME TO FLOURISH

MARCH
march
2022

SUNDAY	MONDAY	TUESDAY	WEDNESDAY
		1	2
6	7	8	9
13	14	15	16
20	21	22	23
27	28	29	30

THURSDAY	FRIDAY	SATURDAY
3	4	5
10	11	12
17	18	19
24	25	26
31		

Highlight of the day

1 --
2 --
3 --
4 --
5 --
6 --
7 --
8 --
9 --
10 ---
11 ---
12 ---
13 ---
14 ---
15 ---
16 ---
17 ---
18 ---
19 ---
20 ---
21 ---
22 ---
23 ---
24 ---
25 ---
26 ---
27 ---
28 ---
29 ---
30 ---
31 ---

AFFIRMATION
board

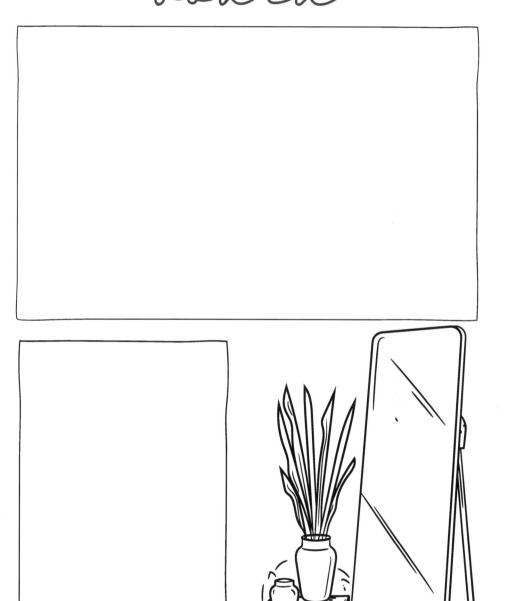

Monthly Sleep Tracker

	PM						AM														**PM**					
1	**7**	**8**	**9**	**10**	**11**	12	1	2	3	4	5	6	7	8	9	10	11	**12**	**1**	**2**	**3**	**4**	**5**	**6**		
2	**7**	**8**	**9**	**10**	**11**	12	1	2	3	4	5	6	7	8	9	10	11	**12**	**1**	**2**	**3**	**4**	**5**	**6**		
3	**7**	**8**	**9**	**10**	**11**	12	1	2	3	4	5	6	7	8	9	10	11	**12**	**1**	**2**	**3**	**4**	**5**	**6**		
4	**7**	**8**	**9**	**10**	**11**	12	1	2	3	4	5	6	7	8	9	10	11	**12**	**1**	**2**	**3**	**4**	**5**	**6**		
5	**7**	**8**	**9**	**10**	**11**	12	1	2	3	4	5	6	7	8	9	10	11	**12**	**1**	**2**	**3**	**4**	**5**	**6**		
6	**7**	**8**	**9**	**10**	**11**	12	1	2	3	4	5	6	7	8	9	10	11	**12**	**1**	**2**	**3**	**4**	**5**	**6**		
7	**7**	**8**	**9**	**10**	**11**	12	1	2	3	4	5	6	7	8	9	10	11	**12**	**1**	**2**	**3**	**4**	**5**	**6**		
8	**7**	**8**	**9**	**10**	**11**	12	1	2	3	4	5	6	7	8	9	10	11	**12**	**1**	**2**	**3**	**4**	**5**	**6**		
9	**7**	**8**	**9**	**10**	**11**	12	1	2	3	4	5	6	7	8	9	10	11	**12**	**1**	**2**	**3**	**4**	**5**	**6**		
10	**7**	**8**	**9**	**10**	**11**	12	1	2	3	4	5	6	7	8	9	10	11	**12**	**1**	**2**	**3**	**4**	**5**	**6**		
11	**7**	**8**	**9**	**10**	**11**	12	1	2	3	4	5	6	7	8	9	10	11	**12**	**1**	**2**	**3**	**4**	**5**	**6**		
12	**7**	**8**	**9**	**10**	**11**	12	1	2	3	4	5	6	7	8	9	10	11	**12**	**1**	**2**	**3**	**4**	**5**	**6**		
13	**7**	**8**	**9**	**10**	**11**	12	1	2	3	4	5	6	7	8	9	10	11	**12**	**1**	**2**	**3**	**4**	**5**	**6**		
14	**7**	**8**	**9**	**10**	**11**	12	1	2	3	4	5	6	7	8	9	10	11	**12**	**1**	**2**	**3**	**4**	**5**	**6**		
15	**7**	**8**	**9**	**10**	**11**	12	1	2	3	4	5	6	7	8	9	10	11	**12**	**1**	**2**	**3**	**4**	**5**	**6**		
16	**7**	**8**	**9**	**10**	**11**	12	1	2	3	4	5	6	7	8	9	10	11	**12**	**1**	**2**	**3**	**4**	**5**	**6**		
17	**7**	**8**	**9**	**10**	**11**	12	1	2	3	4	5	6	7	8	9	10	11	**12**	**1**	**2**	**3**	**4**	**5**	**6**		
18	**7**	**8**	**9**	**10**	**11**	12	1	2	3	4	5	6	7	8	9	10	11	**12**	**1**	**2**	**3**	**4**	**5**	**6**		
19	**7**	**8**	**9**	**10**	**11**	12	1	2	3	4	5	6	7	8	9	10	11	**12**	**1**	**2**	**3**	**4**	**5**	**6**		
20	**7**	**8**	**9**	**10**	**11**	12	1	2	3	4	5	6	7	8	9	10	11	**12**	**1**	**2**	**3**	**4**	**5**	**6**		
21	**7**	**8**	**9**	**10**	**11**	12	1	2	3	4	5	6	7	8	9	10	11	**12**	**1**	**2**	**3**	**4**	**5**	**6**		
22	**7**	**8**	**9**	**10**	**11**	12	1	2	3	4	5	6	7	8	9	10	11	**12**	**1**	**2**	**3**	**4**	**5**	**6**		
23	**7**	**8**	**9**	**10**	**11**	12	1	2	3	4	5	6	7	8	9	10	11	**12**	**1**	**2**	**3**	**4**	**5**	**6**		
24	**7**	**8**	**9**	**10**	**11**	12	1	2	3	4	5	6	7	8	9	10	11	**12**	**1**	**2**	**3**	**4**	**5**	**6**		
25	**7**	**8**	**9**	**10**	**11**	12	1	2	3	4	5	6	7	8	9	10	11	**12**	**1**	**2**	**3**	**4**	**5**	**6**		
26	**7**	**8**	**9**	**10**	**11**	12	1	2	3	4	5	6	7	8	9	10	11	**12**	**1**	**2**	**3**	**4**	**5**	**6**		
27	**7**	**8**	**9**	**10**	**11**	12	1	2	3	4	5	6	7	8	9	10	11	**12**	**1**	**2**	**3**	**4**	**5**	**6**		
28	**7**	**8**	**9**	**10**	**11**	12	1	2	3	4	5	6	7	8	9	10	11	**12**	**1**	**2**	**3**	**4**	**5**	**6**		
29	**7**	**8**	**9**	**10**	**11**	12	1	2	3	4	5	6	7	8	9	10	11	**12**	**1**	**2**	**3**	**4**	**5**	**6**		
30	**7**	**8**	**9**	**10**	**11**	12	1	2	3	4	5	6	7	8	9	10	11	**12**	**1**	**2**	**3**	**4**	**5**	**6**		
31	**7**	**8**	**9**	**10**	**11**	12	1	2	3	4	5	6	7	8	9	10	11	**12**	**1**	**2**	**3**	**4**	**5**	**6**		

THINGS TO
remember

Mood Tracker

○ Happy   ○ Sad   ○ Grumpy   ○ Energetic

○ Calm   ○ Anxious   ○ Angry   ○

○ Normal   ○ Sick   ○ Tired   ○

SELF-CARE

routine

Body

Mind

Soul

Water yourself like you would a houseplant

Water Log

COLOUR KEY

 :

 :

 :

 :

1
2
3
4
5
6
7
8
9
10
11
12
13
14
15
16
17
18
19
20
21
22
23
24
25
26
27
28
29
30
31

PLAYLIST
march

ON REPEAT

Habit Tracker

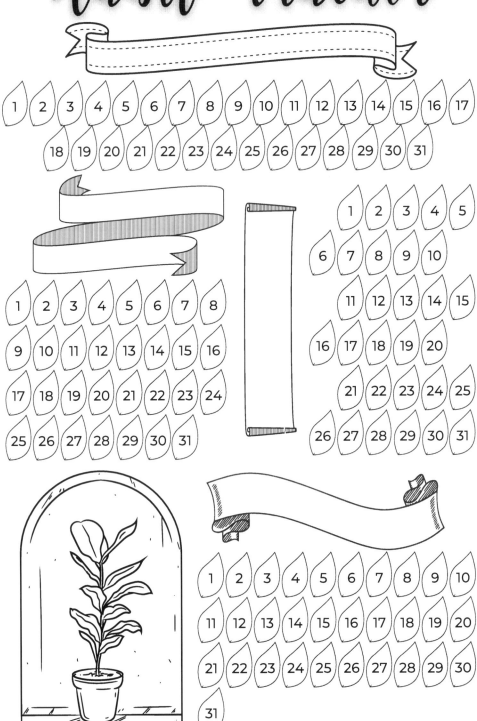

1 2 3 4 5 6 7 8 9 10 11 12 13 14 15 16 17
18 19 20 21 22 23 24 25 26 27 28 29 30 31

1 2 3 4 5 6 7 8
9 10 11 12 13 14 15 16
17 18 19 20 21 22 23 24
25 26 27 28 29 30 31

1 2 3 4 5
6 7 8 9 10
11 12 13 14 15
16 17 18 19 20
21 22 23 24 25
26 27 28 29 30 31

1 2 3 4 5 6 7 8 9 10
11 12 13 14 15 16 17 18 19 20
21 22 23 24 25 26 27 28 29 30
31

TO-DO LIST
march

NO.	TO DO	Y / N

NOTES

Gratitude Log

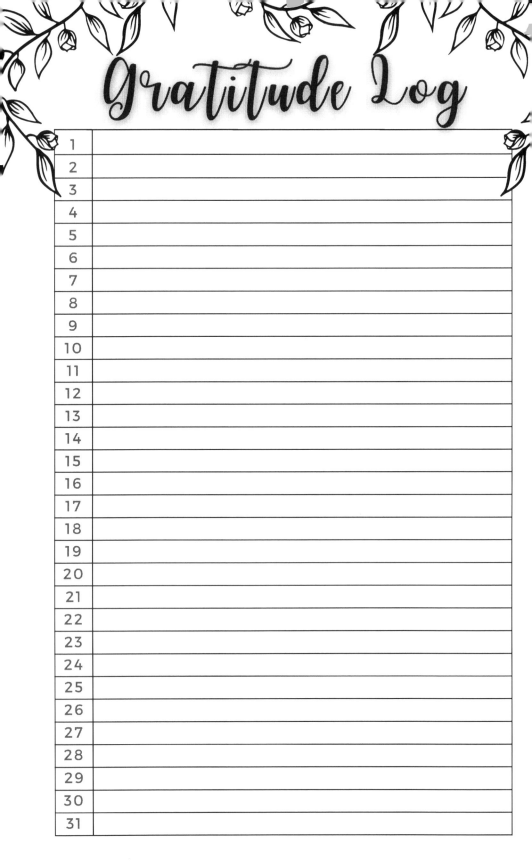

1	
2	
3	
4	
5	
6	
7	
8	
9	
10	
11	
12	
13	
14	
15	
16	
17	
18	
19	
20	
21	
22	
23	
24	
25	
26	
27	
28	
29	
30	
31	

VISION
board

MY NOTES

MY DOODLES

April

I AM EXACTLY WHERE I AM MEANT TO BEE

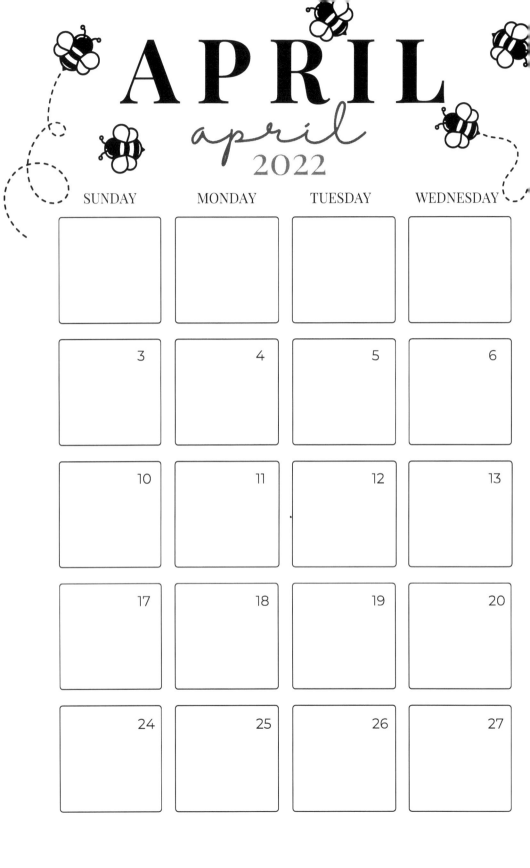

APRIL
april
2022

SUNDAY	MONDAY	TUESDAY	WEDNESDAY
3	4	5	6
10	11	12	13
17	18	19	20
24	25	26	27

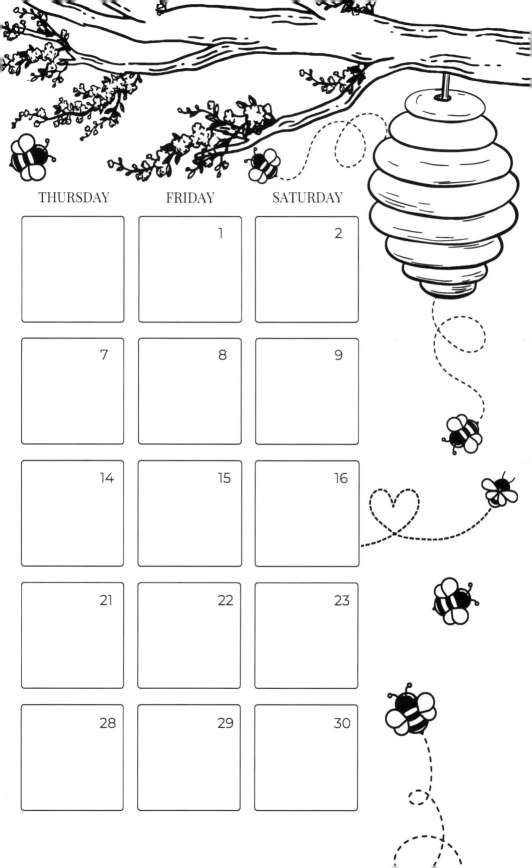

THURSDAY	FRIDAY	SATURDAY
	1	2
7	8	9
14	15	16
21	22	23
28	29	30

Highlight of the day

1 --
2 --
3 --
4 --
5 --
6 --
7 --
8 --
9 --
10 ---------------------------------------
11 ---------------------------------------
12 ---------------------------------------
13 ---------------------------------------
14 ---------------------------------------
15 ---------------------------------------
16 ---------------------------------------
17 ---------------------------------------
18 ---------------------------------------
19 ---------------------------------------
20 ---------------------------------------
21 ---------------------------------------
22 ---------------------------------------
23 ---------------------------------------
24 ---------------------------------------
25 ---------------------------------------
26 ---------------------------------------
27 ---------------------------------------
28 ---------------------------------------
29 ---------------------------------------
30 ---------------------------------------

AFFIRMATION
board

Monthly Sleep Tracker

	PM					AM																PM					
1	7	8	9	10	11	12	1	2	3	4	5	6	7	8	9	10	11	12	1	2	3	4	5	6
2	7	8	9	10	11	12	1	2	3	4	5	6	7	8	9	10	11	12	1	2	3	4	5	6
3	7	8	9	10	11	12	1	2	3	4	5	6	7	8	9	10	11	12	1	2	3	4	5	6
4	7	8	9	10	11	12	1	2	3	4	5	6	7	8	9	10	11	12	1	2	3	4	5	6
5	7	8	9	10	11	12	1	2	3	4	5	6	7	8	9	10	11	12	1	2	3	4	5	6
6	7	8	9	10	11	12	1	2	3	4	5	6	7	8	9	10	11	12	1	2	3	4	5	6
7	7	8	9	10	11	12	1	2	3	4	5	6	7	8	9	10	11	12	1	2	3	4	5	6
8	7	8	9	10	11	12	1	2	3	4	5	6	7	8	9	10	11	12	1	2	3	4	5	6
9	7	8	9	10	11	12	1	2	3	4	5	6	7	8	9	10	11	12	1	2	3	4	5	6
10	7	8	9	10	11	12	1	2	3	4	5	6	7	8	9	10	11	12	1	2	3	4	5	6
11	7	8	9	10	11	12	1	2	3	4	5	6	7	8	9	10	11	12	1	2	3	4	5	6
12	7	8	9	10	11	12	1	2	3	4	5	6	7	8	9	10	11	12	1	2	3	4	5	6
13	7	8	9	10	11	12	1	2	3	4	5	6	7	8	9	10	11	12	1	2	3	4	5	6
14	7	8	9	10	11	12	1	2	3	4	5	6	7	8	9	10	11	12	1	2	3	4	5	6
15	7	8	9	10	11	12	1	2	3	4	5	6	7	8	9	10	11	12	1	2	3	4	5	6
16	7	8	9	10	11	12	1	2	3	4	5	6	7	8	9	10	11	12	1	2	3	4	5	6
17	7	8	9	10	11	12	1	2	3	4	5	6	7	8	9	10	11	12	1	2	3	4	5	6
18	7	8	9	10	11	12	1	2	3	4	5	6	7	8	9	10	11	12	1	2	3	4	5	6
19	7	8	9	10	11	12	1	2	3	4	5	6	7	8	9	10	11	12	1	2	3	4	5	6
20	7	8	9	10	11	12	1	2	3	4	5	6	7	8	9	10	11	12	1	2	3	4	5	6
21	7	8	9	10	11	12	1	2	3	4	5	6	7	8	9	10	11	12	1	2	3	4	5	6
22	7	8	9	10	11	12	1	2	3	4	5	6	7	8	9	10	11	12	1	2	3	4	5	6
23	7	8	9	10	11	12	1	2	3	4	5	6	7	8	9	10	11	12	1	2	3	4	5	6
24	7	8	9	10	11	12	1	2	3	4	5	6	7	8	9	10	11	12	1	2	3	4	5	6
25	7	8	9	10	11	12	1	2	3	4	5	6	7	8	9	10	11	12	1	2	3	4	5	6
26	7	8	9	10	11	12	1	2	3	4	5	6	7	8	9	10	11	12	1	2	3	4	5	6
27	7	8	9	10	11	12	1	2	3	4	5	6	7	8	9	10	11	12	1	2	3	4	5	6
28	7	8	9	10	11	12	1	2	3	4	5	6	7	8	9	10	11	12	1	2	3	4	5	6
29	7	8	9	10	11	12	1	2	3	4	5	6	7	8	9	10	11	12	1	2	3	4	5	6
30	7	8	9	10	11	12	1	2	3	4	5	6	7	8	9	10	11	12	1	2	3	4	5	6

THINGS TO
remember

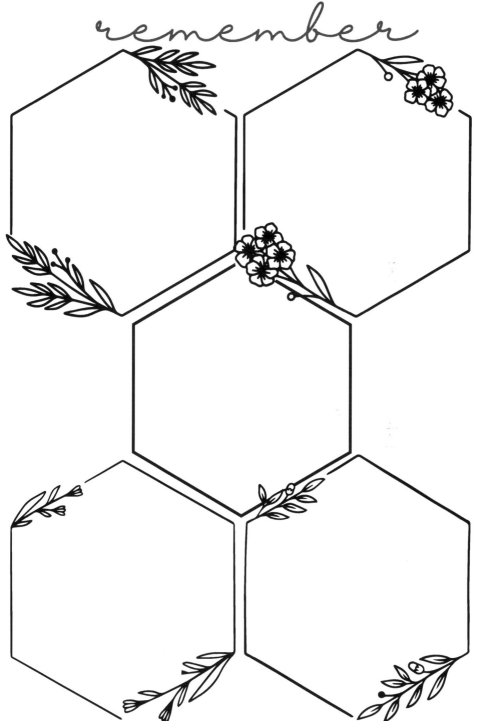

Mood Tracker

1 2 3 4 5 6 7 8 9 10 11 12 13 14 15 16 17 18 19 20 21 22 23 24 25 26 27 28 29 30

○ Happy ○ Sad ○ Grumpy ○ Energetic
○ Calm ○ Anxious ○ Angry ○
○ Normal ○ Sick ○ Tired ○

SELF-CARE
routine

Body

Mind

Soul

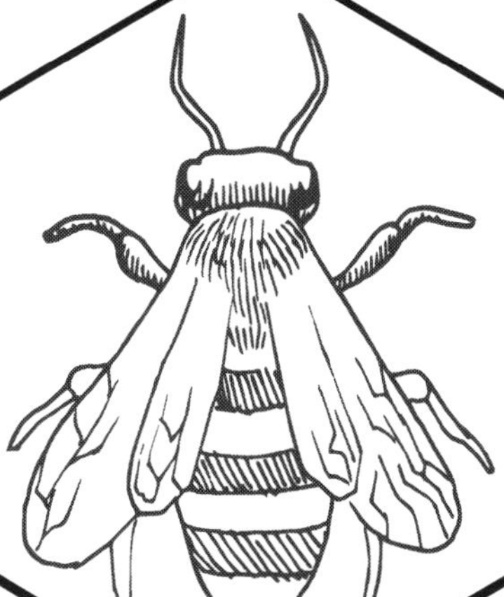

Water Log

COLOUR KEY

 :

 :

 :

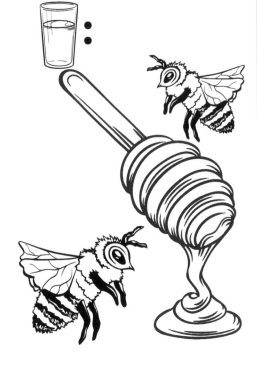 :

1
2
3
4
5
6
7
8
9
10
11
12
13
14
15
16
17
18
19
20
21
22
23
24
25
26
27
28
29
30

PLAYLIST
april

ON REPEAT

TO-DO LIST
april

NO.	TO DO	Y / N

NOTES	

Gratitude Log

1	
2	
3	
4	
5	
6	
7	
8	
9	
10	
11	
12	
13	
14	
15	
16	
17	
18	
19	
20	
21	
22	
23	
24	
25	
26	
27	
28	
29	
30	

VISION
board

MY NOTES

MY DOODLES

THE UNIVERSE WILL MAKE IT HAPPEN

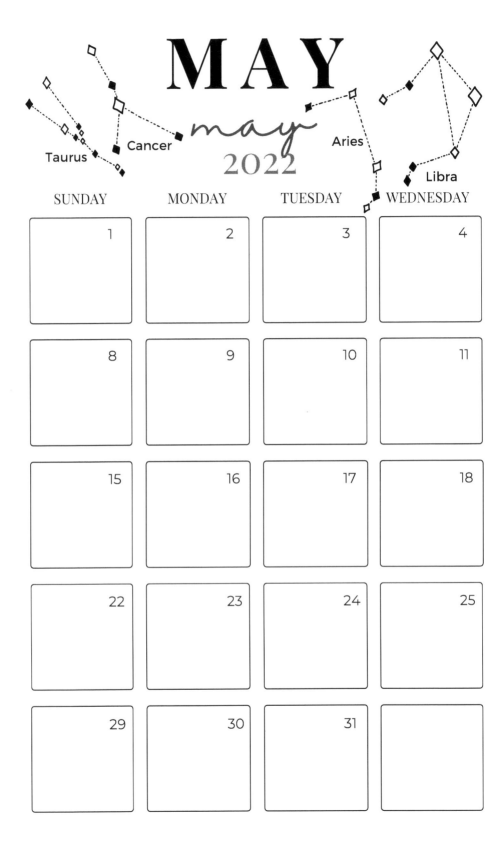

MAY

may
2022

Taurus Cancer Aries Libra

SUNDAY	MONDAY	TUESDAY	WEDNESDAY
1	2	3	4
8	9	10	11
15	16	17	18
22	23	24	25
29	30	31	

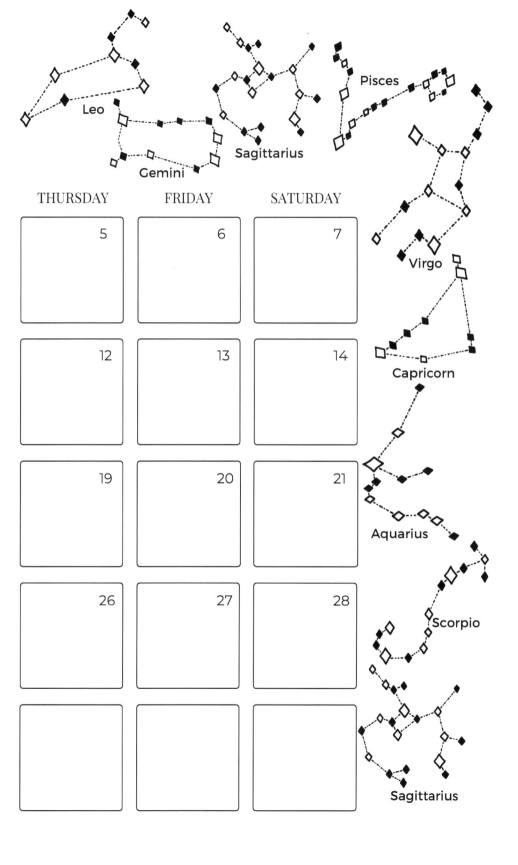

THURSDAY	FRIDAY	SATURDAY
5	6	7
12	13	14
19	20	21
26	27	28

Highlight of the day

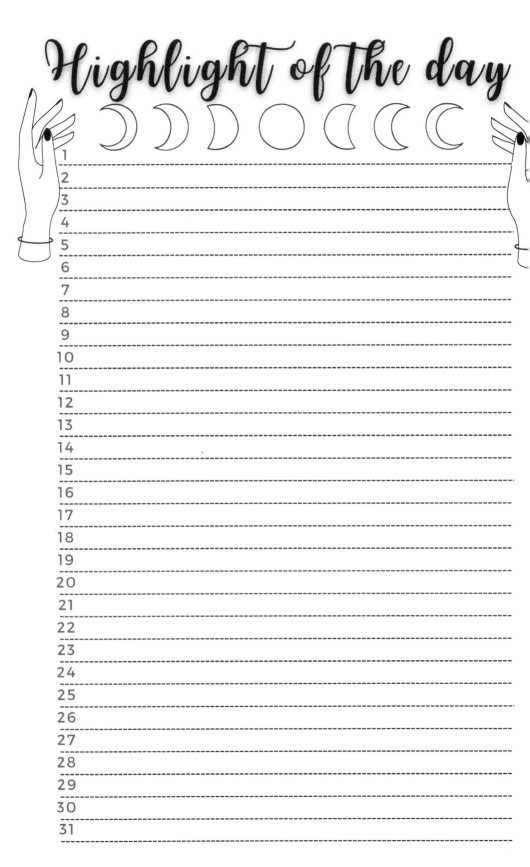

1
2
3
4
5
6
7
8
9
10
11
12
13
14
15
16
17
18
19
20
21
22
23
24
25
26
27
28
29
30
31

AFFIRMATION

board

THE WORLD IS AT MY *fingertips*

Monthly Sleep Tracker

	PM					AM														PM						
1	7	8	9	10	11	12	1	2	3	4	5	6	7	8	9	10	11	12	1	2	3	4	5	6
2	7	8	9	10	11	12	1	2	3	4	5	6	7	8	9	10	11	12	1	2	3	4	5	6
3	7	8	9	10	11	12	1	2	3	4	5	6	7	8	9	10	11	12	1	2	3	4	5	6
4	7	8	9	10	11	12	1	2	3	4	5	6	7	8	9	10	11	12	1	2	3	4	5	6
5	7	8	9	10	11	12	1	2	3	4	5	6	7	8	9	10	11	12	1	2	3	4	5	6
6	7	8	9	10	11	12	1	2	3	4	5	6	7	8	9	10	11	12	1	2	3	4	5	6
7	7	8	9	10	11	12	1	2	3	4	5	6	7	8	9	10	11	12	1	2	3	4	5	6
8	7	8	9	10	11	12	1	2	3	4	5	6	7	8	9	10	11	12	1	2	3	4	5	6
9	7	8	9	10	11	12	1	2	3	4	5	6	7	8	9	10	11	12	1	2	3	4	5	6
10	7	8	9	10	11	12	1	2	3	4	5	6	7	8	9	10	11	12	1	2	3	4	5	6
11	7	8	9	10	11	12	1	2	3	4	5	6	7	8	9	10	11	12	1	2	3	4	5	6
12	7	8	9	10	11	12	1	2	3	4	5	6	7	8	9	10	11	12	1	2	3	4	5	6
13	7	8	9	10	11	12	1	2	3	4	5	6	7	8	9	10	11	12	1	2	3	4	5	6
14	7	8	9	10	11	12	1	2	3	4	5	6	7	8	9	10	11	12	1	2	3	4	5	6
15	7	8	9	10	11	12	1	2	3	4	5	6	7	8	9	10	11	12	1	2	3	4	5	6
16	7	8	9	10	11	12	1	2	3	4	5	6	7	8	9	10	11	12	1	2	3	4	5	6
17	7	8	9	10	11	12	1	2	3	4	5	6	7	8	9	10	11	12	1	2	3	4	5	6
18	7	8	9	10	11	12	1	2	3	4	5	6	7	8	9	10	11	12	1	2	3	4	5	6
19	7	8	9	10	11	12	1	2	3	4	5	6	7	8	9	10	11	12	1	2	3	4	5	6
20	7	8	9	10	11	12	1	2	3	4	5	6	7	8	9	10	11	12	1	2	3	4	5	6
21	7	8	9	10	11	12	1	2	3	4	5	6	7	8	9	10	11	12	1	2	3	4	5	6
22	7	8	9	10	11	12	1	2	3	4	5	6	7	8	9	10	11	12	1	2	3	4	5	6
23	7	8	9	10	11	12	1	2	3	4	5	6	7	8	9	10	11	12	1	2	3	4	5	6
24	7	8	9	10	11	12	1	2	3	4	5	6	7	8	9	10	11	12	1	2	3	4	5	6
25	7	8	9	10	11	12	1	2	3	4	5	6	7	8	9	10	11	12	1	2	3	4	5	6
26	7	8	9	10	11	12	1	2	3	4	5	6	7	8	9	10	11	12	1	2	3	4	5	6
27	7	8	9	10	11	12	1	2	3	4	5	6	7	8	9	10	11	12	1	2	3	4	5	6
28	7	8	9	10	11	12	1	2	3	4	5	6	7	8	9	10	11	12	1	2	3	4	5	6
29	7	8	9	10	11	12	1	2	3	4	5	6	7	8	9	10	11	12	1	2	3	4	5	6
30	7	8	9	10	11	12	1	2	3	4	5	6	7	8	9	10	11	12	1	2	3	4	5	6
31	7	8	9	10	11	12	1	2	3	4	5	6	7	8	9	10	11	12	1	2	3	4	5	6

THINGS TO
remember

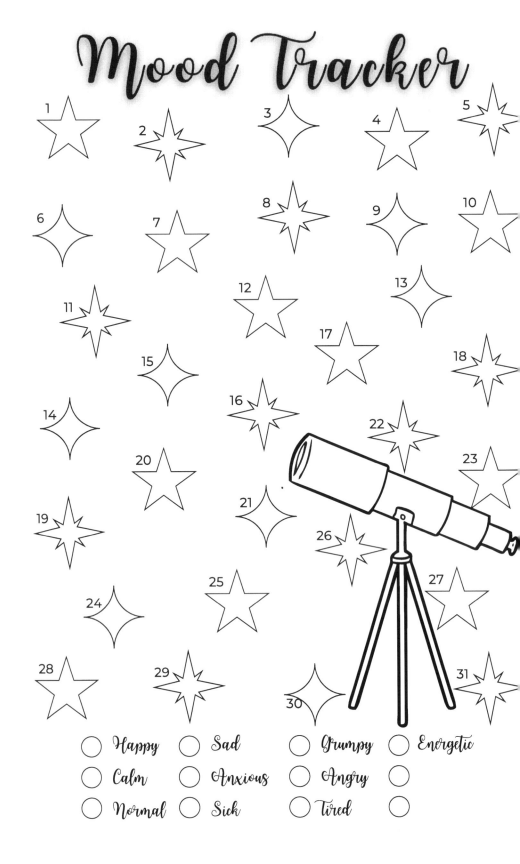

SELF-CARE

routine

Body

Mind

Soul

Water Log

COLOUR KEY

 :

 :

 :

 :

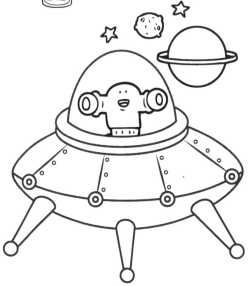

1
2
3
4
5
6
7
8
9
10
11
12
13
14
15
16
17
18
19
20
21
22
23
24
25
26
27
28
29
30
31

PLAYLIST

may

ON REPEAT

Habit Tracker

Section 1:
1 2 3 4 5 6
7 8 9 10 11 12
13 14 15 16 17 18 19
20 21 22 23 24 25
26 27 28 29 30 31

Section 2:
1
2 3
4 5 6 7
8 9 10 11 12
13 14 15 16 17 18
19 20 21 22 23
24 25 26 27
28 29 30 31

Section 3:
1 2 3 4 5 6 7 8 9 10 11 12
13 14 15 16 17 18 19 20 21 22 23 24
25 26 27 28 29 30 31

Section 4:
1 2 3 4 5
6 7 8 9 10
11 12 13 14 15
16 17 18 19 20
21 22 23 24 25
26 27 28 29 30 31

TO-DO LIST

may

NO.	TO DO	Y / N

NOTES

Gratitude Log

1	
2	
3	
4	
5	
6	
7	
8	
9	
10	
11	
12	
13	
14	
15	
16	
17	
18	
19	
20	
21	
22	
23	
24	
25	
26	
27	
28	
29	
30	
31	

VISION
board

MY NOTES

MY DOODLES

LIVE YOUR LIFE WITH ZEST

JUNE

june

2022

SUNDAY	MONDAY	TUESDAY	WEDNESDAY
			1
5	6	7	8
12	13	14	15
19	20	21	22
26	27	28	29

THURSDAY	FRIDAY	SATURDAY
2	3	4
9	10	11
16	17	18
23	24	25
30		

Highlight of the day

1 --
2 --
3 --
4 --
5 --
6 --
7 --
8 --
9 --
10 --
11 --
12 --
13 --
14 --
15 --
16 --
17 --
18 --
19 --
20 --
21 --
22 --
23 --
24 --
25 --
26 --
27 --
28 --
29 --
30 --

AFFIRMATION
board

Monthly Sleep Tracker

	PM						AM															**PM**						
1	**7**	**8**	**9**	**10**	**11**	12	1	2	3	4	5	6	7	8	9	10	11	**12**	1	2	3	4	5	6
2	**7**	**8**	**9**	**10**	**11**	12	1	2	3	4	5	6	7	8	9	10	11	**12**	1	2	3	4	5	6
3	**7**	**8**	**9**	**10**	**11**	12	1	2	3	4	5	6	7	8	9	10	11	**12**	1	2	3	4	5	6
4	**7**	**8**	**9**	**10**	**11**	12	1	2	3	4	5	6	7	8	9	10	11	**12**	1	2	3	4	5	6
5	**7**	**8**	**9**	**10**	**11**	12	1	2	3	4	5	6	7	8	9	10	11	**12**	1	2	3	4	5	6
6	**7**	**8**	**9**	**10**	**11**	12	1	2	3	4	5	6	7	8	9	10	11	**12**	1	2	3	4	5	6
7	**7**	**8**	**9**	**10**	**11**	12	1	2	3	4	5	6	7	8	9	10	11	**12**	1	2	3	4	5	6
8	**7**	**8**	**9**	**10**	**11**	12	1	2	3	4	5	6	7	8	9	10	11	**12**	1	2	3	4	5	6
9	**7**	**8**	**9**	**10**	**11**	12	1	2	3	4	5	6	7	8	9	10	11	**12**	1	2	3	4	5	6
10	**7**	**8**	**9**	**10**	**11**	12	1	2	3	4	5	6	7	8	9	10	11	**12**	1	2	3	4	5	6
11	**7**	**8**	**9**	**10**	**11**	12	1	2	3	4	5	6	7	8	9	10	11	**12**	1	2	3	4	5	6
12	**7**	**8**	**9**	**10**	**11**	12	1	2	3	4	5	6	7	8	9	10	11	**12**	1	2	3	4	5	6
13	**7**	**8**	**9**	**10**	**11**	12	1	2	3	4	5	6	7	8	9	10	11	**12**	1	2	3	4	5	6
14	**7**	**8**	**9**	**10**	**11**	12	1	2	3	4	5	6	7	8	9	10	11	**12**	1	2	3	4	5	6
15	**7**	**8**	**9**	**10**	**11**	12	1	2	3	4	5	6	7	8	9	10	11	**12**	1	2	3	4	5	6
16	**7**	**8**	**9**	**10**	**11**	12	1	2	3	4	5	6	7	8	9	10	11	**12**	1	2	3	4	5	6
17	**7**	**8**	**9**	**10**	**11**	12	1	2	3	4	5	6	7	8	9	10	11	**12**	1	2	3	4	5	6
18	**7**	**8**	**9**	**10**	**11**	12	1	2	3	4	5	6	7	8	9	10	11	**12**	1	2	3	4	5	6
19	**7**	**8**	**9**	**10**	**11**	12	1	2	3	4	5	6	7	8	9	10	11	**12**	1	2	3	4	5	6
20	**7**	**8**	**9**	**10**	**11**	12	1	2	3	4	5	6	7	8	9	10	11	**12**	1	2	3	4	5	6
21	**7**	**8**	**9**	**10**	**11**	12	1	2	3	4	5	6	7	8	9	10	11	**12**	1	2	3	4	5	6
22	**7**	**8**	**9**	**10**	**11**	12	1	2	3	4	5	6	7	8	9	10	11	**12**	1	2	3	4	5	6
23	**7**	**8**	**9**	**10**	**11**	12	1	2	3	4	5	6	7	8	9	10	11	**12**	1	2	3	4	5	6
24	**7**	**8**	**9**	**10**	**11**	12	1	2	3	4	5	6	7	8	9	10	11	**12**	1	2	3	4	5	6
25	**7**	**8**	**9**	**10**	**11**	12	1	2	3	4	5	6	7	8	9	10	11	**12**	1	2	3	4	5	6
26	**7**	**8**	**9**	**10**	**11**	12	1	2	3	4	5	6	7	8	9	10	11	**12**	1	2	3	4	5	6
27	**7**	**8**	**9**	**10**	**11**	12	1	2	3	4	5	6	7	8	9	10	11	**12**	1	2	3	4	5	6
28	**7**	**8**	**9**	**10**	**11**	12	1	2	3	4	5	6	7	8	9	10	11	**12**	1	2	3	4	5	6
29	**7**	**8**	**9**	**10**	**11**	12	1	2	3	4	5	6	7	8	9	10	11	**12**	1	2	3	4	5	6
30	**7**	**8**	**9**	**10**	**11**	12	1	2	3	4	5	6	7	8	9	10	11	**12**	1	2	3	4	5	6

THINGS TO
remember

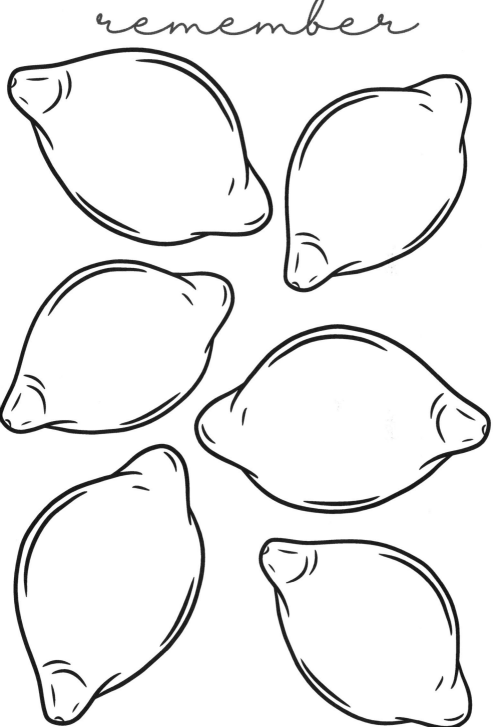

Mood Tracker

○ *Happy* ○ *Sad* ○ *Grumpy* ○ *Energetic*

○ *Calm* ○ *Anxious* ○ *Angry* ○

○ *Normal* ○ *Sick* ○ *Tired* ○

SELF-CARE
routine

Body | Mind

Soul

RELAX
&
unwind

Water Log

COLOUR KEY

	1
	2
	3
	4
	5
	6
	7
	8
	9
	10
	11
	12
	13
	14
	15
	16
	17
	18
	19
	20
	21
	22
	23
	24
	25
	26
	27
	28
	29
	30

PLAYLIST

june

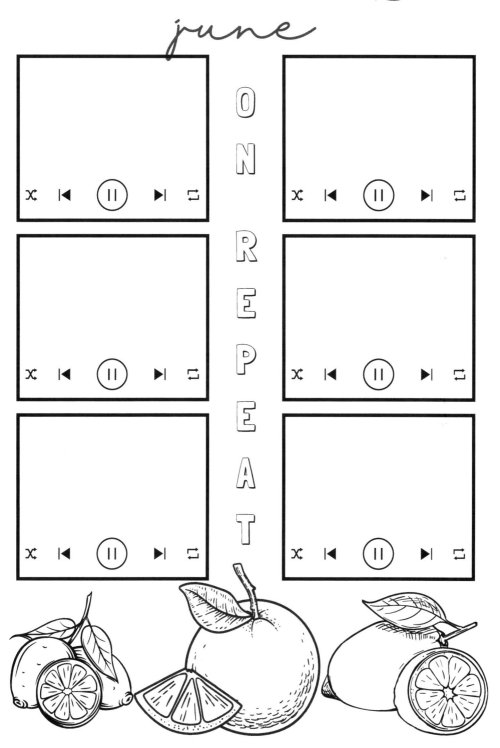

ON REPEAT

Habit Tracker

TO-DO LIST
june

NO.	TO DO	Y / N

NOTES

Gratitude Log

1	
2	
3	
4	
5	
6	
7	
8	
9	
10	
11	
12	
13	
14	
15	
16	
17	
18	
19	
20	
21	
22	
23	
24	
25	
26	
27	
28	
29	
30	

VISION
board

MY NOTES

MY DOODLES

JULY.
july
2022

SUNDAY	MONDAY	TUESDAY	WEDNESDAY
3	4	5	6
10	11	12	13
17	18	19	20
24	25	26	27
31			

THURSDAY	FRIDAY	SATURDAY
	1	2
7	8	9
14	15	16
21	22	23
28	29	30

Highlight of the day

1
2
3
4
5
6
7
8
9
10
11
12
13
14
15
16
17
18
19
20
21
22
23
24
25
26
27
28
29
30
31

AFFIRMATION
board

THE WORLD IS MY *oyster*

Monthly Sleep Tracker

	PM						AM														PM						
1	7	8	9	10	11	12	1	2	3	4	5	6	7	8	9	10	11	12	1	2	3	4	5	6
2	7	8	9	10	11	12	1	2	3	4	5	6	7	8	9	10	11	12	1	2	3	4	5	6
3	7	8	9	10	11	12	1	2	3	4	5	6	7	8	9	10	11	12	1	2	3	4	5	6
4	7	8	9	10	11	12	1	2	3	4	5	6	7	8	9	10	11	12	1	2	3	4	5	6
5	7	8	9	10	11	12	1	2	3	4	5	6	7	8	9	10	11	12	1	2	3	4	5	6
6	7	8	9	10	11	12	1	2	3	4	5	6	7	8	9	10	11	12	1	2	3	4	5	6
7	7	8	9	10	11	12	1	2	3	4	5	6	7	8	9	10	11	12	1	2	3	4	5	6
8	7	8	9	10	11	12	1	2	3	4	5	6	7	8	9	10	11	12	1	2	3	4	5	6
9	7	8	9	10	11	12	1	2	3	4	5	6	7	8	9	10	11	12	1	2	3	4	5	6
10	7	8	9	10	11	12	1	2	3	4	5	6	7	8	9	10	11	12	1	2	3	4	5	6
11	7	8	9	10	11	12	1	2	3	4	5	6	7	8	9	10	11	12	1	2	3	4	5	6
12	7	8	9	10	11	12	1	2	3	4	5	6	7	8	9	10	11	12	1	2	3	4	5	6
13	7	8	9	10	11	12	1	2	3	4	5	6	7	8	9	10	11	12	1	2	3	4	5	6
14	7	8	9	10	11	12	1	2	3	4	5	6	7	8	9	10	11	12	1	2	3	4	5	6
15	7	8	9	10	11	12	1	2	3	4	5	6	7	8	9	10	11	12	1	2	3	4	5	6
16	7	8	9	10	11	12	1	2	3	4	5	6	7	8	9	10	11	12	1	2	3	4	5	6
17	7	8	9	10	11	12	1	2	3	4	5	6	7	8	9	10	11	12	1	2	3	4	5	6
18	7	8	9	10	11	12	1	2	3	4	5	6	7	8	9	10	11	12	1	2	3	4	5	6
19	7	8	9	10	11	12	1	2	3	4	5	6	7	8	9	10	11	12	1	2	3	4	5	6
20	7	8	9	10	11	12	1	2	3	4	5	6	7	8	9	10	11	12	1	2	3	4	5	6
21	7	8	9	10	11	12	1	2	3	4	5	6	7	8	9	10	11	12	1	2	3	4	5	6
22	7	8	9	10	11	12	1	2	3	4	5	6	7	8	9	10	11	12	1	2	3	4	5	6
23	7	8	9	10	11	12	1	2	3	4	5	6	7	8	9	10	11	12	1	2	3	4	5	6
24	7	8	9	10	11	12	1	2	3	4	5	6	7	8	9	10	11	12	1	2	3	4	5	6
25	7	8	9	10	11	12	1	2	3	4	5	6	7	8	9	10	11	12	1	2	3	4	5	6
26	7	8	9	10	11	12	1	2	3	4	5	6	7	8	9	10	11	12	1	2	3	4	5	6
27	7	8	9	10	11	12	1	2	3	4	5	6	7	8	9	10	11	12	1	2	3	4	5	6
28	7	8	9	10	11	12	1	2	3	4	5	6	7	8	9	10	11	12	1	2	3	4	5	6
29	7	8	9	10	11	12	1	2	3	4	5	6	7	8	9	10	11	12	1	2	3	4	5	6
30	7	8	9	10	11	12	1	2	3	4	5	6	7	8	9	10	11	12	1	2	3	4	5	6
31	7	8	9	10	11	12	1	2	3	4	5	6	7	8	9	10	11	12	1	2	3	4	5	6

THINGS TO
remember

SELF-CARE
routine

Water Log

COLOUR KEY

- 🥤 :
- 🥤 :
- 🥤 :
- 🥤 :

1
2
3
4
5
6
7
8
9
10
11
12
13
14
15
16
17
18
19
20
21
22
23
24
25
26
27
28
29
30
31

PLAYLIST

july

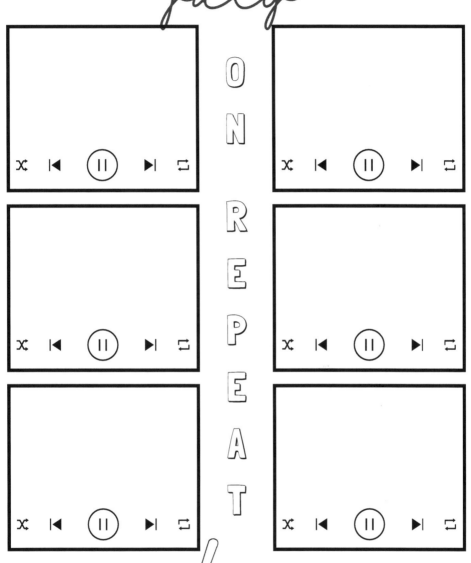

ON REPEAT

Habit Tracker

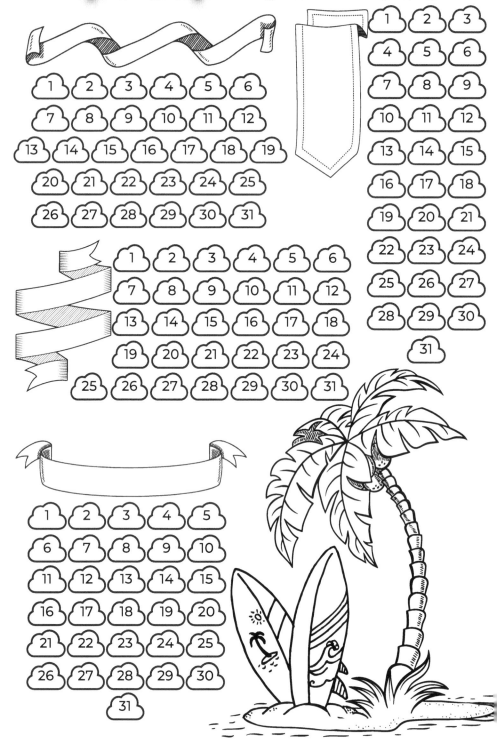

Tracker 1:
1 2 3 4 5 6
7 8 9 10 11 12
13 14 15 16 17 18 19
20 21 22 23 24 25
26 27 28 29 30 31

Tracker 2:
1 2 3
4 5 6
7 8 9
10 11 12
13 14 15
16 17 18
19 20 21
22 23 24
25 26 27
28 29 30
31

Tracker 3:
1 2 3 4 5 6
7 8 9 10 11 12
13 14 15 16 17 18
19 20 21 22 23 24
25 26 27 28 29 30 31

Tracker 4:
1 2 3 4 5
6 7 8 9 10
11 12 13 14 15
16 17 18 19 20
21 22 23 24 25
26 27 28 29 30
31

TO-DO LIST
july

NO.	TO DO	Y / N

NOTES

Gratitude Log

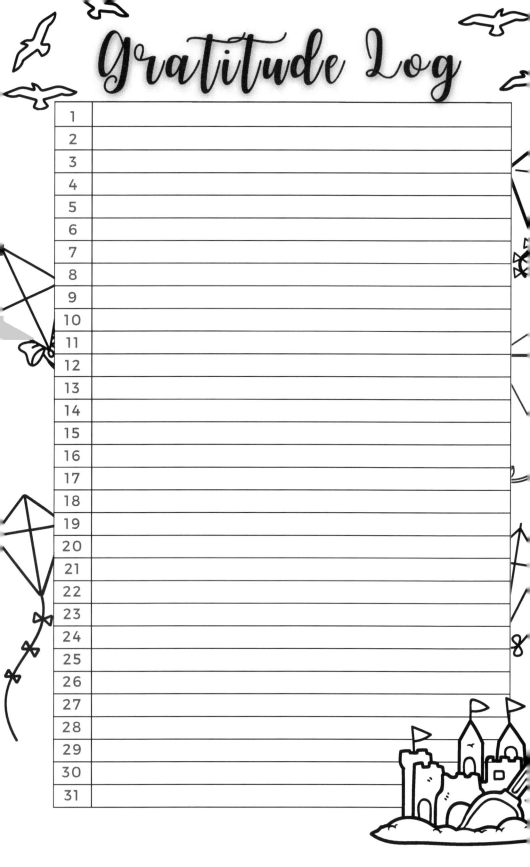

1	
2	
3	
4	
5	
6	
7	
8	
9	
10	
11	
12	
13	
14	
15	
16	
17	
18	
19	
20	
21	
22	
23	
24	
25	
26	
27	
28	
29	
30	
31	

VISION
board

MY NOTES

MY DOODLES

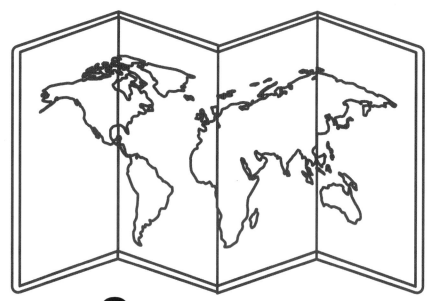

August

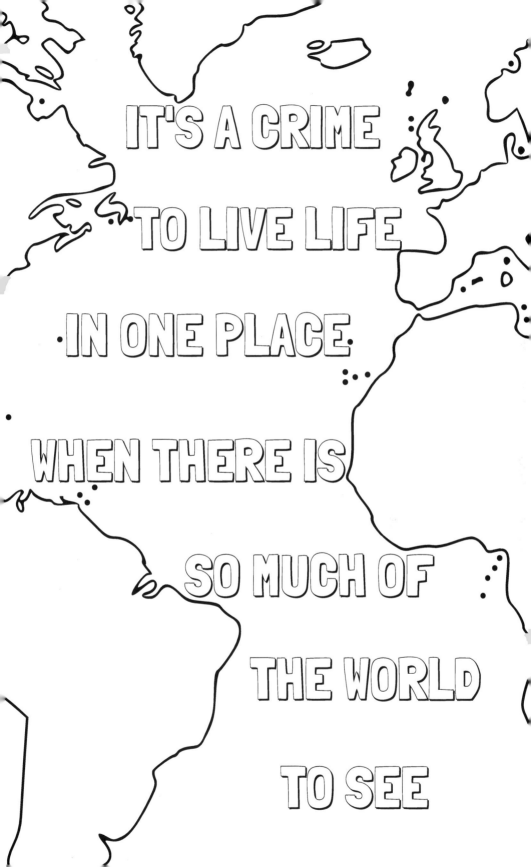

IT'S A CRIME
TO LIVE LIFE
IN ONE PLACE.
WHEN THERE IS
SO MUCH OF
THE WORLD
TO SEE

AUGUST
august
2022

SUNDAY	MONDAY	TUESDAY	WEDNESDAY
	1	2	3
7	8	9	10
14	15	16	17
21	22	23	24
28	29	30	31

THURSDAY	FRIDAY	SATURDAY
4	5	6
11	12	13
18	19	20
25	26	27

Highlight of the day

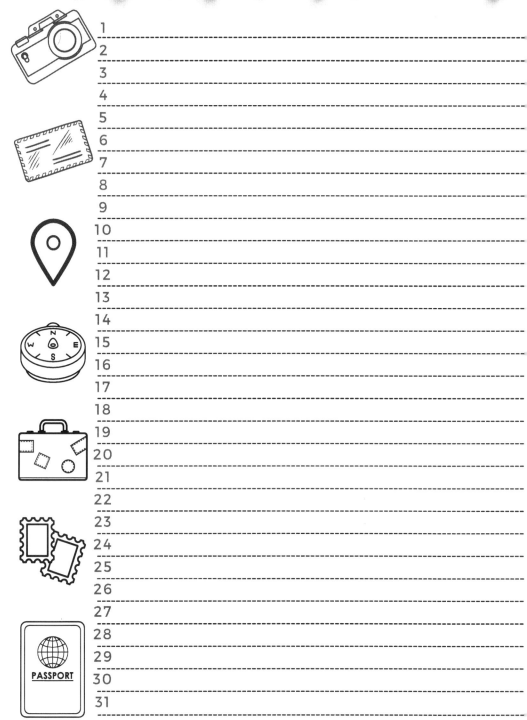

1
2
3
4
5
6
7
8
9
10
11
12
13
14
15
16
17
18
19
20
21
22
23
24
25
26
27
28
29
30
31

AFFIRMATION
board

Monthly Sleep Tracker

	PM					AM																	PM						
1	**7**	**8**	**9**	**10**	**11**	12	1	2	3	4	5	6	7	8	9	10	11	**12**	**1**	**2**	**3**	**4**	**5**	**6**
2	**7**	**8**	**9**	**10**	**11**	12	1	2	3	4	5	6	7	8	9	10	11	**12**	**1**	**2**	**3**	**4**	**5**	**6**
3	**7**	**8**	**9**	**10**	**11**	12	1	2	3	4	5	6	7	8	9	10	11	**12**	**1**	**2**	**3**	**4**	**5**	**6**
4	**7**	**8**	**9**	**10**	**11**	12	1	2	3	4	5	6	7	8	9	10	11	**12**	**1**	**2**	**3**	**4**	**5**	**6**
5	**7**	**8**	**9**	**10**	**11**	12	1	2	3	4	5	6	7	8	9	10	11	**12**	**1**	**2**	**3**	**4**	**5**	**6**
6	**7**	**8**	**9**	**10**	**11**	12	1	2	3	4	5	6	7	8	9	10	11	**12**	**1**	**2**	**3**	**4**	**5**	**6**
7	**7**	**8**	**9**	**10**	**11**	12	1	2	3	4	5	6	7	8	9	10	11	**12**	**1**	**2**	**3**	**4**	**5**	**6**
8	**7**	**8**	**9**	**10**	**11**	12	1	2	3	4	5	6	7	8	9	10	11	**12**	**1**	**2**	**3**	**4**	**5**	**6**
9	**7**	**8**	**9**	**10**	**11**	12	1	2	3	4	5	6	7	8	9	10	11	**12**	**1**	**2**	**3**	**4**	**5**	**6**
10	**7**	**8**	**9**	**10**	**11**	12	1	2	3	4	5	6	7	8	9	10	11	**12**	**1**	**2**	**3**	**4**	**5**	**6**
11	**7**	**8**	**9**	**10**	**11**	12	1	2	3	4	5	6	7	8	9	10	11	**12**	**1**	**2**	**3**	**4**	**5**	**6**
12	**7**	**8**	**9**	**10**	**11**	12	1	2	3	4	5	6	7	8	9	10	11	**12**	**1**	**2**	**3**	**4**	**5**	**6**
13	**7**	**8**	**9**	**10**	**11**	12	1	2	3	4	5	6	7	8	9	10	11	**12**	**1**	**2**	**3**	**4**	**5**	**6**
14	**7**	**8**	**9**	**10**	**11**	12	1	2	3	4	5	6	7	8	9	10	11	**12**	**1**	**2**	**3**	**4**	**5**	**6**
15	**7**	**8**	**9**	**10**	**11**	12	1	2	3	4	5	6	7	8	9	10	11	**12**	**1**	**2**	**3**	**4**	**5**	**6**
16	**7**	**8**	**9**	**10**	**11**	12	1	2	3	4	5	6	7	8	9	10	11	**12**	**1**	**2**	**3**	**4**	**5**	**6**
17	**7**	**8**	**9**	**10**	**11**	12	1	2	3	4	5	6	7	8	9	10	11	**12**	**1**	**2**	**3**	**4**	**5**	**6**
18	**7**	**8**	**9**	**10**	**11**	12	1	2	3	4	5	6	7	8	9	10	11	**12**	**1**	**2**	**3**	**4**	**5**	**6**
19	**7**	**8**	**9**	**10**	**11**	12	1	2	3	4	5	6	7	8	9	10	11	**12**	**1**	**2**	**3**	**4**	**5**	**6**
20	**7**	**8**	**9**	**10**	**11**	12	1	2	3	4	5	6	7	8	9	10	11	**12**	**1**	**2**	**3**	**4**	**5**	**6**
21	**7**	**8**	**9**	**10**	**11**	12	1	2	3	4	5	6	7	8	9	10	11	**12**	**1**	**2**	**3**	**4**	**5**	**6**
22	**7**	**8**	**9**	**10**	**11**	12	1	2	3	4	5	6	7	8	9	10	11	**12**	**1**	**2**	**3**	**4**	**5**	**6**
23	**7**	**8**	**9**	**10**	**11**	12	1	2	3	4	5	6	7	8	9	10	11	**12**	**1**	**2**	**3**	**4**	**5**	**6**
24	**7**	**8**	**9**	**10**	**11**	12	1	2	3	4	5	6	7	8	9	10	11	**12**	**1**	**2**	**3**	**4**	**5**	**6**
25	**7**	**8**	**9**	**10**	**11**	12	1	2	3	4	5	6	7	8	9	10	11	**12**	**1**	**2**	**3**	**4**	**5**	**6**
26	**7**	**8**	**9**	**10**	**11**	12	1	2	3	4	5	6	7	8	9	10	11	**12**	**1**	**2**	**3**	**4**	**5**	**6**
27	**7**	**8**	**9**	**10**	**11**	12	1	2	3	4	5	6	7	8	9	10	11	**12**	**1**	**2**	**3**	**4**	**5**	**6**
28	**7**	**8**	**9**	**10**	**11**	12	1	2	3	4	5	6	7	8	9	10	11	**12**	**1**	**2**	**3**	**4**	**5**	**6**
29	**7**	**8**	**9**	**10**	**11**	12	1	2	3	4	5	6	7	8	9	10	11	**12**	**1**	**2**	**3**	**4**	**5**	**6**
30	**7**	**8**	**9**	**10**	**11**	12	1	2	3	4	5	6	7	8	9	10	11	**12**	**1**	**2**	**3**	**4**	**5**	**6**
31	**7**	**8**	**9**	**10**	**11**	12	1	2	3	4	5	6	7	8	9	10	11	**12**	**1**	**2**	**3**	**4**	**5**	**6**

THINGS TO
remember

Mood Tracker

○ Happy   ○ Sad   ○ Grumpy   ○ Energetic

○ Calm   ○ Anxious   ○ Angry   ○

○ Normal   ○ Sick   ○ Tired   ○

SELF-CARE
routine

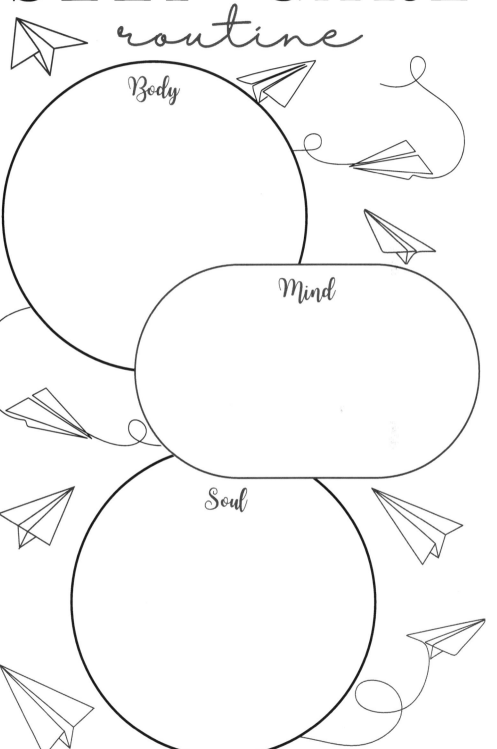

Body

Mind

Soul

Water Log

COLOUR KEY

 :

 :

 :

 :

1
2
3
4
5
6
7
8
9
10
11
12
13
14
15
16
17
18
19
20
21
22
23
24
25
26
27
28
29
30
31

PLAYLIST
august

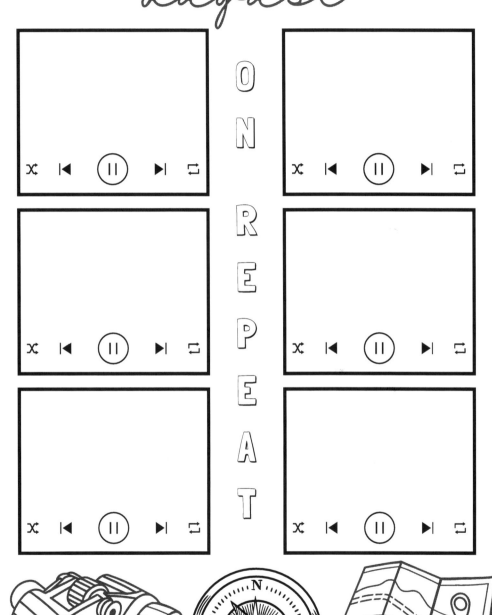

ON REPEAT

Habit Tracker

1
2 3
4 5 6
7 8 9 10
11 12 13 14 15 16
17 18 19 20 21 22 23
24 25 26 27 28 29 30 31

1
2 3 4
5 6 7
8 9 10
11 12 13
14 15 16
17 18 19
20 21 22
23 24 25
26 27 28
29 30 31

1 2 3 4 5 6 7 8 9 10
11 12 13 14 15 16 17 18 19 20
21 22 23 24 25 26 27 28 29 30
31

1 2 3 4 5 6
7 8 9 10 11 12
13 14 15 16 17 18 19
20 21 22 23 24 25
26 27 28 29 30 31

TO-DO LIST
august

NO.	TO DO	Y / N

NOTES	

Gratitude Log

1	
2	
3	
4	
5	
6	
7	
8	
9	
10	
11	
12	
13	
14	
15	
16	
17	
18	
19	
20	
21	
22	
23	
24	
25	
26	
27	
28	
29	
30	
31	

VISION
board

MY NOTES

MY DOODLES

START FROM THE GROUND UP

SEPTEMBER

september

2022

SUNDAY	MONDAY	TUESDAY	WEDNESDAY
4	5	6	7
11	12	13	14
18	19	20	21
25	26	27	28

THURSDAY	FRIDAY	SATURDAY
1	2	3
8	9	10
15	16	17
22	23	24
29	30	

Highlight of the day

1
2
3
4
5
6
7
8
9
10
11
12
13
14
15
16
17
18
19
20
21
22
23
24
25
26
27
28
29
30

AFFIRMATION
board

Monthly Sleep Tracker

	PM					AM														PM						
1	**7**	**8**	**9**	**10**	**11**	12	1	2	3	4	5	6	7	8	9	10	11	**12**	**1**	**2**	**3**	**4**	**5**	**6**
2	**7**	**8**	**9**	**10**	**11**	12	1	2	3	4	5	6	7	8	9	10	11	**12**	**1**	**2**	**3**	**4**	**5**	**6**
3	**7**	**8**	**9**	**10**	**11**	12	1	2	3	4	5	6	7	8	9	10	11	**12**	**1**	**2**	**3**	**4**	**5**	**6**
4	**7**	**8**	**9**	**10**	**11**	12	1	2	3	4	5	6	7	8	9	10	11	**12**	**1**	**2**	**3**	**4**	**5**	**6**
5	**7**	**8**	**9**	**10**	**11**	12	1	2	3	4	5	6	7	8	9	10	11	**12**	**1**	**2**	**3**	**4**	**5**	**6**
6	**7**	**8**	**9**	**10**	**11**	12	1	2	3	4	5	6	7	8	9	10	11	**12**	**1**	**2**	**3**	**4**	**5**	**6**
7	**7**	**8**	**9**	**10**	**11**	12	1	2	3	4	5	6	7	8	9	10	11	**12**	**1**	**2**	**3**	**4**	**5**	**6**
8	**7**	**8**	**9**	**10**	**11**	12	1	2	3	4	5	6	7	8	9	10	11	**12**	**1**	**2**	**3**	**4**	**5**	**6**
9	**7**	**8**	**9**	**10**	**11**	12	1	2	3	4	5	6	7	8	9	10	11	**12**	**1**	**2**	**3**	**4**	**5**	**6**
10	**7**	**8**	**9**	**10**	**11**	12	1	2	3	4	5	6	7	8	9	10	11	**12**	**1**	**2**	**3**	**4**	**5**	**6**
11	**7**	**8**	**9**	**10**	**11**	12	1	2	3	4	5	6	7	8	9	10	11	**12**	**1**	**2**	**3**	**4**	**5**	**6**
12	**7**	**8**	**9**	**10**	**11**	12	1	2	3	4	5	6	7	8	9	10	11	**12**	**1**	**2**	**3**	**4**	**5**	**6**
13	**7**	**8**	**9**	**10**	**11**	12	1	2	3	4	5	6	7	8	9	10	11	**12**	**1**	**2**	**3**	**4**	**5**	**6**
14	**7**	**8**	**9**	**10**	**11**	12	1	2	3	4	5	6	7	8	9	10	11	**12**	**1**	**2**	**3**	**4**	**5**	**6**
15	**7**	**8**	**9**	**10**	**11**	12	1	2	3	4	5	6	7	8	9	10	11	**12**	**1**	**2**	**3**	**4**	**5**	**6**
16	**7**	**8**	**9**	**10**	**11**	12	1	2	3	4	5	6	7	8	9	10	11	**12**	**1**	**2**	**3**	**4**	**5**	**6**
17	**7**	**8**	**9**	**10**	**11**	12	1	2	3	4	5	6	7	8	9	10	11	**12**	**1**	**2**	**3**	**4**	**5**	**6**
18	**7**	**8**	**9**	**10**	**11**	12	1	2	3	4	5	6	7	8	9	10	11	**12**	**1**	**2**	**3**	**4**	**5**	**6**
19	**7**	**8**	**9**	**10**	**11**	12	1	2	3	4	5	6	7	8	9	10	11	**12**	**1**	**2**	**3**	**4**	**5**	**6**
20	**7**	**8**	**9**	**10**	**11**	12	1	2	3	4	5	6	7	8	9	10	11	**12**	**1**	**2**	**3**	**4**	**5**	**6**
21	**7**	**8**	**9**	**10**	**11**	12	1	2	3	4	5	6	7	8	9	10	11	**12**	**1**	**2**	**3**	**4**	**5**	**6**
22	**7**	**8**	**9**	**10**	**11**	12	1	2	3	4	5	6	7	8	9	10	11	**12**	**1**	**2**	**3**	**4**	**5**	**6**
23	**7**	**8**	**9**	**10**	**11**	12	1	2	3	4	5	6	7	8	9	10	11	**12**	**1**	**2**	**3**	**4**	**5**	**6**
24	**7**	**8**	**9**	**10**	**11**	12	1	2	3	4	5	6	7	8	9	10	11	**12**	**1**	**2**	**3**	**4**	**5**	**6**
25	**7**	**8**	**9**	**10**	**11**	12	1	2	3	4	5	6	7	8	9	10	11	**12**	**1**	**2**	**3**	**4**	**5**	**6**
26	**7**	**8**	**9**	**10**	**11**	12	1	2	3	4	5	6	7	8	9	10	11	**12**	**1**	**2**	**3**	**4**	**5**	**6**
27	**7**	**8**	**9**	**10**	**11**	12	1	2	3	4	5	6	7	8	9	10	11	**12**	**1**	**2**	**3**	**4**	**5**	**6**
28	**7**	**8**	**9**	**10**	**11**	12	1	2	3	4	5	6	7	8	9	10	11	**12**	**1**	**2**	**3**	**4**	**5**	**6**
29	**7**	**8**	**9**	**10**	**11**	12	1	2	3	4	5	6	7	8	9	10	11	**12**	**1**	**2**	**3**	**4**	**5**	**6**
30	**7**	**8**	**9**	**10**	**11**	12	1	2	3	4	5	6	7	8	9	10	11	**12**	**1**	**2**	**3**	**4**	**5**	**6**

THINGS TO
remember

Mood Tracker

- ○ Happy
- ○ Sad
- ○ Grumpy
- ○ Energetic
- ○ Calm
- ○ Anxious
- ○ Angry
- ○
- ○ Normal
- ○ Sick
- ○ Tired
- ○

SELF-CARE
routine

Mind

Body

Soul

Water Log

COLOUR KEY

 :

 :

 :

 :

1
2
3
4
5
6
7
8
9
10
11
12
13
14
15
16
17
18
19
20
21
22
23
24
25
26
27
28
29
30

PLAYLIST

september

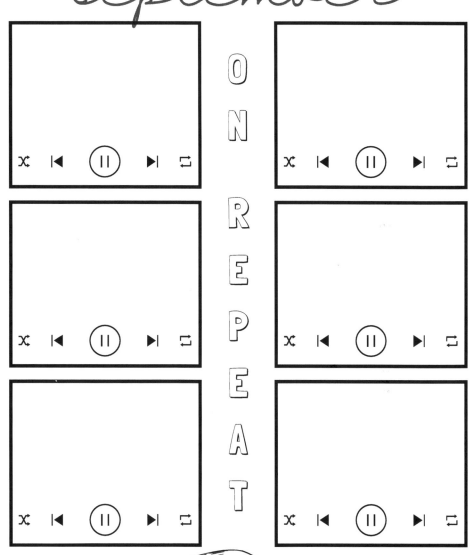

ON REPEAT

Habit Tracker

TO-DO LIST
september

NO.	TO DO	Y / N

NOTES

Gratitude Log

1	
2	
3	
4	
5	
6	
7	
8	
9	
10	
11	
12	
13	
14	
15	
16	
17	
18	
19	
20	
21	
22	
23	
24	
25	
26	
27	
28	
29	
30	

VISION
board

MY NOTES

MY DOODLES

OCTOBER

october

2022

SUNDAY	MONDAY	TUESDAY	WEDNESDAY
2	3	4	5
9	10	11	12
16	17	18	19
23	24	25	26
30	31		

THURSDAY	FRIDAY	SATURDAY
		1
6	7	8
13	14	15
20	21	22
27	28	29

Highlight of the day

1
2
3
4
5
6
7
8
9
10
11
12
13
14
15
16
17
18
19
20
21
22
23
24
25
26
27
28
29
30
31

AFFIRMATION
board

Monthly Sleep Tracker

	PM					AM														PM					
1	**7**	**8**	**9**	**10**	**11**	12	1	2	3	4	5	6	7	8	9	10	11	**12**	**1**	**2**	**3**	**4**	**5**	**6**
2	**7**	**8**	**9**	**10**	**11**	12	1	2	3	4	5	6	7	8	9	10	11	**12**	**1**	**2**	**3**	**4**	**5**	**6**
3	**7**	**8**	**9**	**10**	**11**	12	1	2	3	4	5	6	7	8	9	10	11	**12**	**1**	**2**	**3**	**4**	**5**	**6**
4	**7**	**8**	**9**	**10**	**11**	12	1	2	3	4	5	6	7	8	9	10	11	**12**	**1**	**2**	**3**	**4**	**5**	**6**
5	**7**	**8**	**9**	**10**	**11**	12	1	2	3	4	5	6	7	8	9	10	11	**12**	**1**	**2**	**3**	**4**	**5**	**6**
6	**7**	**8**	**9**	**10**	**11**	12	1	2	3	4	5	6	7	8	9	10	11	**12**	**1**	**2**	**3**	**4**	**5**	**6**
7	**7**	**8**	**9**	**10**	**11**	12	1	2	3	4	5	6	7	8	9	10	11	**12**	**1**	**2**	**3**	**4**	**5**	**6**
8	**7**	**8**	**9**	**10**	**11**	12	1	2	3	4	5	6	7	8	9	10	11	**12**	**1**	**2**	**3**	**4**	**5**	**6**
9	**7**	**8**	**9**	**10**	**11**	12	1	2	3	4	5	6	7	8	9	10	11	**12**	**1**	**2**	**3**	**4**	**5**	**6**
10	**7**	**8**	**9**	**10**	**11**	12	1	2	3	4	5	6	7	8	9	10	11	**12**	**1**	**2**	**3**	**4**	**5**	**6**
11	**7**	**8**	**9**	**10**	**11**	12	1	2	3	4	5	6	7	8	9	10	11	**12**	**1**	**2**	**3**	**4**	**5**	**6**
12	**7**	**8**	**9**	**10**	**11**	12	1	2	3	4	5	6	7	8	9	10	11	**12**	**1**	**2**	**3**	**4**	**5**	**6**
13	**7**	**8**	**9**	**10**	**11**	12	1	2	3	4	5	6	7	8	9	10	11	**12**	**1**	**2**	**3**	**4**	**5**	**6**
14	**7**	**8**	**9**	**10**	**11**	12	1	2	3	4	5	6	7	8	9	10	11	**12**	**1**	**2**	**3**	**4**	**5**	**6**
15	**7**	**8**	**9**	**10**	**11**	12	1	2	3	4	5	6	7	8	9	10	11	**12**	**1**	**2**	**3**	**4**	**5**	**6**
16	**7**	**8**	**9**	**10**	**11**	12	1	2	3	4	5	6	7	8	9	10	11	**12**	**1**	**2**	**3**	**4**	**5**	**6**
17	**7**	**8**	**9**	**10**	**11**	12	1	2	3	4	5	6	7	8	9	10	11	**12**	**1**	**2**	**3**	**4**	**5**	**6**
18	**7**	**8**	**9**	**10**	**11**	12	1	2	3	4	5	6	7	8	9	10	11	**12**	**1**	**2**	**3**	**4**	**5**	**6**
19	**7**	**8**	**9**	**10**	**11**	12	1	2	3	4	5	6	7	8	9	10	11	**12**	**1**	**2**	**3**	**4**	**5**	**6**
20	**7**	**8**	**9**	**10**	**11**	12	1	2	3	4	5	6	7	8	9	10	11	**12**	**1**	**2**	**3**	**4**	**5**	**6**
21	**7**	**8**	**9**	**10**	**11**	12	1	2	3	4	5	6	7	8	9	10	11	**12**	**1**	**2**	**3**	**4**	**5**	**6**
22	**7**	**8**	**9**	**10**	**11**	12	1	2	3	4	5	6	7	8	9	10	11	**12**	**1**	**2**	**3**	**4**	**5**	**6**
23	**7**	**8**	**9**	**10**	**11**	12	1	2	3	4	5	6	7	8	9	10	11	**12**	**1**	**2**	**3**	**4**	**5**	**6**
24	**7**	**8**	**9**	**10**	**11**	12	1	2	3	4	5	6	7	8	9	10	11	**12**	**1**	**2**	**3**	**4**	**5**	**6**
25	**7**	**8**	**9**	**10**	**11**	12	1	2	3	4	5	6	7	8	9	10	11	**12**	**1**	**2**	**3**	**4**	**5**	**6**
26	**7**	**8**	**9**	**10**	**11**	12	1	2	3	4	5	6	7	8	9	10	11	**12**	**1**	**2**	**3**	**4**	**5**	**6**
27	**7**	**8**	**9**	**10**	**11**	12	1	2	3	4	5	6	7	8	9	10	11	**12**	**1**	**2**	**3**	**4**	**5**	**6**
28	**7**	**8**	**9**	**10**	**11**	12	1	2	3	4	5	6	7	8	9	10	11	**12**	**1**	**2**	**3**	**4**	**5**	**6**
29	**7**	**8**	**9**	**10**	**11**	12	1	2	3	4	5	6	7	8	9	10	11	**12**	**1**	**2**	**3**	**4**	**5**	**6**
30	**7**	**8**	**9**	**10**	**11**	12	1	2	3	4	5	6	7	8	9	10	11	**12**	**1**	**2**	**3**	**4**	**5**	**6**
31	**7**	**8**	**9**	**10**	**11**	12	1	2	3	4	5	6	7	8	9	10	11	**12**	**1**	**2**	**3**	**4**	**5**	**6**

THINGS TO
remember

Mood Tracker

1 2 3 4 5 6
7 8 9 10 11 12
13 14 15 16 17 18
19 20 21 22 23 24
25 26 27 28 29 30 31

○ Happy ○ Sad ○ Grumpy ○ Energetic
○ Calm ○ Anxious ○ Angry ○
○ Normal ○ Sick ○ Tired ○

SELF-CARE
routine

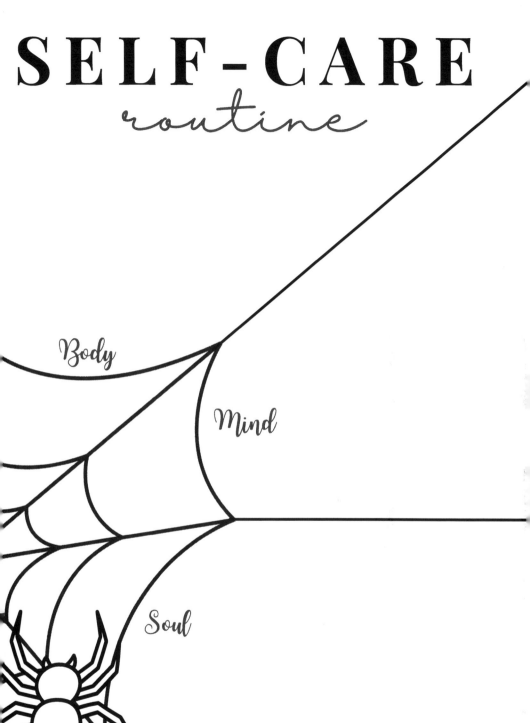

Body

Mind

Soul

Water Log

COLOUR KEY

 :

 :

 :

 :

1
2
3
4
5
6
7
8
9
10
11
12
13
14
15
16
17
18
19
20
21
22
23
24
25
26
27
28
29
30
31

PLAYLIST
october

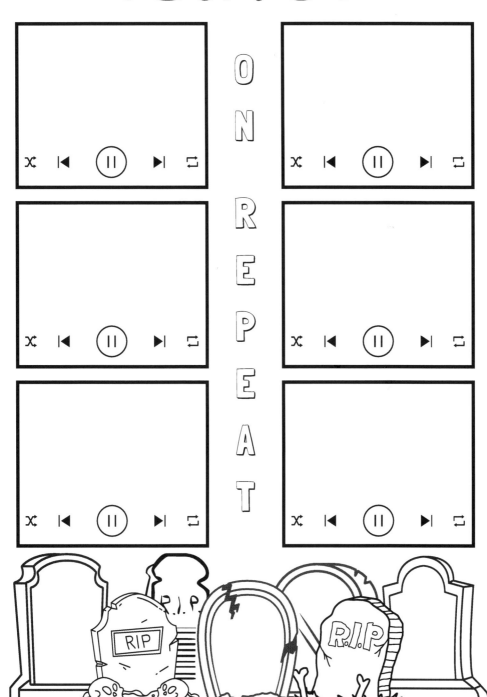

ON REPEAT

Habit Tracker

| 1 | 2 | 3 | 4 | 5 | 6 | 7 | 8 |

| 9 | 10 | 11 | 12 | 13 | 14 | 15 | 16 |

17	18	19	20
21	22	23	24
25	26	27	28
29	30	31

1	2	3	4	5
6	7	8	9	10
11	12	13	14	15
16	17	18	19	20
21	22	23	24	25
26	27	28	29	30
31

1	2
3	4
5	6
7	8
9	10
11	12
13	14
15	16
17	18
19	20
21	22
23	24
25	26
27	28
29	30
31

1	2	3	4	5	6	7	8	9	10
11	12	13	14	15	16	17	18	19	20	21
22	23	24	25	26	27	28	29	30	31

TO-DO LIST
october

NO.	TO DO	Y / N

NOTES	

Gratitude Log

1	
2	
3	
4	
5	
6	
7	
8	
9	
10	
11	
12	
13	
14	
15	
16	
17	
18	
19	
20	
21	
22	
23	
24	
25	
26	
27	
28	
29	
30	
31	

VISION
board

MY NOTES

MY DOODLES

November

NOVEMBER

november

2022

SUNDAY	MONDAY	TUESDAY	WEDNESDAY
		1	2
6	7	8	9
13	14	15	16
20	21	22	23
27	28	29	30

THURSDAY	FRIDAY	SATURDAY
3	4	5
10	11	12
17	18	19
24	25	26

Highlight of the day

1 --
2 --
3 --
4 --
5 --
6 --
7 --
8 --
9 --
10 --
11 --
12 --
13 --
14 --
15 --
16 --
17 --
18 --
19 --
20 --
21 --
22 --
23 --
24 --
25 --
26 --
27 --
28 --
29 --
30 --

AFFIRMATION
board

CAN'T TALK,
--- REVIVING ---
MY SOUL

Monthly Sleep Tracker

	PM						AM													**PM**					
1	**7**	**8**	**9**	**10**	**11**	12	1	2	3	4	5	6	7	8	9	10	11	**12**	**1**	**2**	**3**	**4**	**5**	**6**
2	**7**	**8**	**9**	**10**	**11**	12	1	2	3	4	5	6	7	8	9	10	11	**12**	**1**	**2**	**3**	**4**	**5**	**6**
3	**7**	**8**	**9**	**10**	**11**	12	1	2	3	4	5	6	7	8	9	10	11	**12**	**1**	**2**	**3**	**4**	**5**	**6**
4	**7**	**8**	**9**	**10**	**11**	12	1	2	3	4	5	6	7	8	9	10	11	**12**	**1**	**2**	**3**	**4**	**5**	**6**
5	**7**	**8**	**9**	**10**	**11**	12	1	2	3	4	5	6	7	8	9	10	11	**12**	**1**	**2**	**3**	**4**	**5**	**6**
6	**7**	**8**	**9**	**10**	**11**	12	1	2	3	4	5	6	7	8	9	10	11	**12**	**1**	**2**	**3**	**4**	**5**	**6**
7	**7**	**8**	**9**	**10**	**11**	12	1	2	3	4	5	6	7	8	9	10	11	**12**	**1**	**2**	**3**	**4**	**5**	**6**
8	**7**	**8**	**9**	**10**	**11**	12	1	2	3	4	5	6	7	8	9	10	11	**12**	**1**	**2**	**3**	**4**	**5**	**6**
9	**7**	**8**	**9**	**10**	**11**	12	1	2	3	4	5	6	7	8	9	10	11	**12**	**1**	**2**	**3**	**4**	**5**	**6**
10	**7**	**8**	**9**	**10**	**11**	12	1	2	3	4	5	6	7	8	9	10	11	**12**	**1**	**2**	**3**	**4**	**5**	**6**
11	**7**	**8**	**9**	**10**	**11**	12	1	2	3	4	5	6	7	8	9	10	11	**12**	**1**	**2**	**3**	**4**	**5**	**6**
12	**7**	**8**	**9**	**10**	**11**	12	1	2	3	4	5	6	7	8	9	10	11	**12**	**1**	**2**	**3**	**4**	**5**	**6**
13	**7**	**8**	**9**	**10**	**11**	12	1	2	3	4	5	6	7	8	9	10	11	**12**	**1**	**2**	**3**	**4**	**5**	**6**
14	**7**	**8**	**9**	**10**	**11**	12	1	2	3	4	5	6	7	8	9	10	11	**12**	**1**	**2**	**3**	**4**	**5**	**6**
15	**7**	**8**	**9**	**10**	**11**	12	1	2	3	4	5	6	7	8	9	10	11	**12**	**1**	**2**	**3**	**4**	**5**	**6**
16	**7**	**8**	**9**	**10**	**11**	12	1	2	3	4	5	6	7	8	9	10	11	**12**	**1**	**2**	**3**	**4**	**5**	**6**
17	**7**	**8**	**9**	**10**	**11**	12	1	2	3	4	5	6	7	8	9	10	11	**12**	**1**	**2**	**3**	**4**	**5**	**6**
18	**7**	**8**	**9**	**10**	**11**	12	1	2	3	4	5	6	7	8	9	10	11	**12**	**1**	**2**	**3**	**4**	**5**	**6**
19	**7**	**8**	**9**	**10**	**11**	12	1	2	3	4	5	6	7	8	9	10	11	**12**	**1**	**2**	**3**	**4**	**5**	**6**
20	**7**	**8**	**9**	**10**	**11**	12	1	2	3	4	5	6	7	8	9	10	11	**12**	**1**	**2**	**3**	**4**	**5**	**6**
21	**7**	**8**	**9**	**10**	**11**	12	1	2	3	4	5	6	7	8	9	10	11	**12**	**1**	**2**	**3**	**4**	**5**	**6**
22	**7**	**8**	**9**	**10**	**11**	12	1	2	3	4	5	6	7	8	9	10	11	**12**	**1**	**2**	**3**	**4**	**5**	**6**
23	**7**	**8**	**9**	**10**	**11**	12	1	2	3	4	5	6	7	8	9	10	11	**12**	**1**	**2**	**3**	**4**	**5**	**6**
24	**7**	**8**	**9**	**10**	**11**	12	1	2	3	4	5	6	7	8	9	10	11	**12**	**1**	**2**	**3**	**4**	**5**	**6**
25	**7**	**8**	**9**	**10**	**11**	12	1	2	3	4	5	6	7	8	9	10	11	**12**	**1**	**2**	**3**	**4**	**5**	**6**
26	**7**	**8**	**9**	**10**	**11**	12	1	2	3	4	5	6	7	8	9	10	11	**12**	**1**	**2**	**3**	**4**	**5**	**6**
27	**7**	**8**	**9**	**10**	**11**	12	1	2	3	4	5	6	7	8	9	10	11	**12**	**1**	**2**	**3**	**4**	**5**	**6**
28	**7**	**8**	**9**	**10**	**11**	12	1	2	3	4	5	6	7	8	9	10	11	**12**	**1**	**2**	**3**	**4**	**5**	**6**
29	**7**	**8**	**9**	**10**	**11**	12	1	2	3	4	5	6	7	8	9	10	11	**12**	**1**	**2**	**3**	**4**	**5**	**6**
30	**7**	**8**	**9**	**10**	**11**	12	1	2	3	4	5	6	7	8	9	10	11	**12**	**1**	**2**	**3**	**4**	**5**	**6**

THINGS TO
remember

SELF-CARE
routine

Body

Mind

Soul

Water Log

COLOUR KEY

 :

 :

 :

1
2
3
4
5
6
7
8
9
10
11
12
13
14
15
16
17
18
19
20
21
22
23
24
25
26
27
28
29
30

PLAYLIST
november

O
N

R
E
P
E
A
T

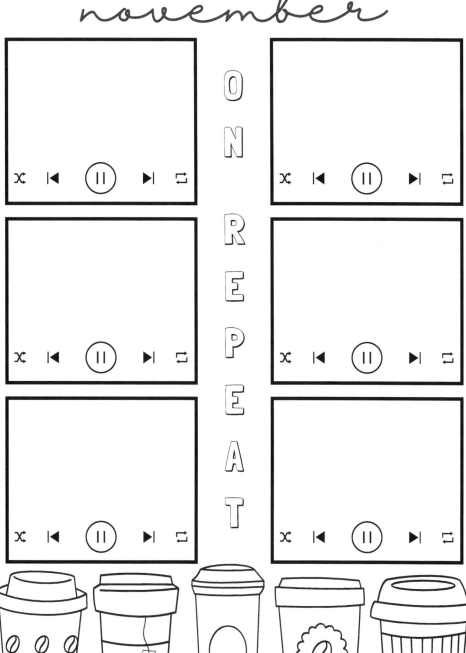

Habit Tracker

| 1 | 2 | 3 | 4 | 5 | 6 | 7 | 8 | 9 | 10 | 11 | 12 | 13 | 14 | 15 |
| 16 | 17 | 18 | 19 | 20 | 21 | 22 | 23 | 24 | 25 | 26 | 27 | 28 | 29 | 30 |

1	2	3	4	5	6
7	8	9	10	11	12
13	14	15	16	17	18	19	20	21
22	23	24	25	26	27	28	29	30

1	2	3	4	5
6	7	8	9	10
11	12	13	14	15
16	17	18	19	20
21	22	23	24	25
26	27	28	29	30

1	2	3	4	5	6	7	8	9	10	11	12	13
14	15	16	17	18	19	20	21	22	23	24
							25	26	27
							28	29	30

TO-DO LIST

november

NO.	TO DO	Y / N

NOTES

Gratitude Log

1	
2	
3	
4	
5	
6	
7	
8	
9	
10	
11	
12	
13	
14	
15	
16	
17	
18	
19	
20	
21	
22	
23	
24	
25	
26	
27	
28	
29	
30	

VISION
board

MY NOTES

MY DOODLES

December

WHAT YOU THINK YOU ARE CAPABLE OF IS ONLY A FRACTION OF WHAT YOU CAN DO

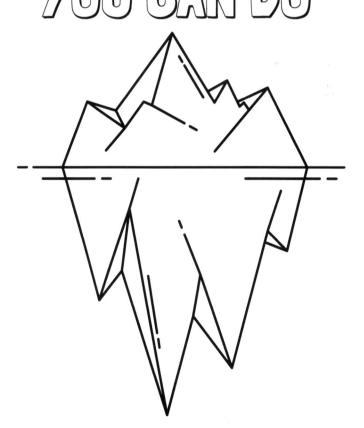

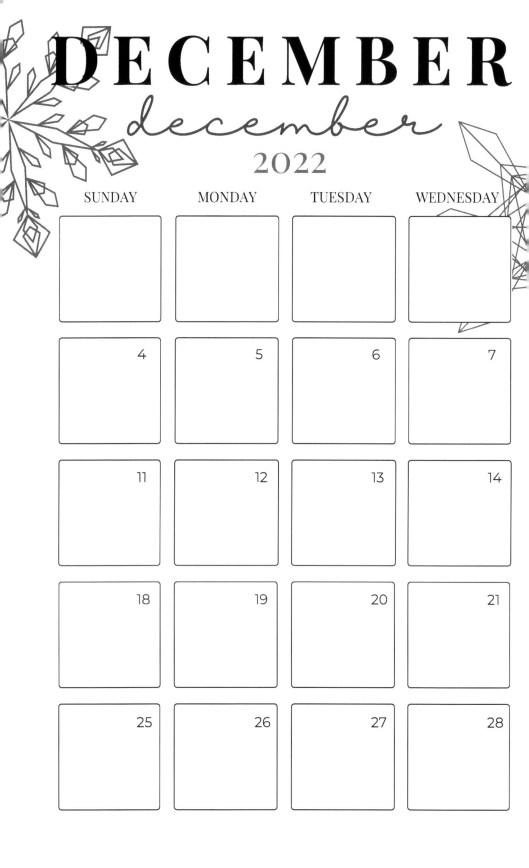

DECEMBER

december

2022

SUNDAY	MONDAY	TUESDAY	WEDNESDAY
4	5	6	7
11	12	13	14
18	19	20	21
25	26	27	28

THURSDAY	FRIDAY	SATURDAY
1	2	3
8	9	10
15	16	17
22	23	24
29	30	31

Highlight of the day

1 --------------------------------
2 --------------------------------
3 --------------------------------
4 --------------------------------
5 --------------------------------
6 --------------------------------
7 --------------------------------
8 --------------------------------
9 --------------------------------
10 --------------------------------
11 --------------------------------
12 --------------------------------
13 --------------------------------
14 --------------------------------
15 --------------------------------
16 --------------------------------
17 --------------------------------
18 --------------------------------
19 --------------------------------
20 --------------------------------
21 --------------------------------
22 --------------------------------
23 --------------------------------
24 --------------------------------
25 --------------------------------
26 --------------------------------
27 --------------------------------
28 --------------------------------
29 --------------------------------
30 --------------------------------
31 --------------------------------

AFFIRMATION
board

Monthly Sleep Tracker

	PM					AM												**PM**					
1	**7**	**8**	**9**	**10**	**11**	12	1	2	3	4	5	6	7	8	9	10	11	**12**	**1**	2	3	4	5	**6**
2	**7**	**8**	**9**	**10**	**11**	12	1	2	3	4	5	6	7	8	9	10	11	**12**	**1**	2	3	4	5	**6**
3	**7**	**8**	**9**	**10**	**11**	12	1	2	3	4	5	6	7	8	9	10	11	**12**	**1**	2	3	4	5	**6**
4	**7**	**8**	**9**	**10**	**11**	12	1	2	3	4	5	6	7	8	9	10	11	**12**	**1**	2	3	4	5	**6**
5	**7**	**8**	**9**	**10**	**11**	12	1	2	3	4	5	6	7	8	9	10	11	**12**	**1**	2	3	4	5	**6**
6	**7**	**8**	**9**	**10**	**11**	12	1	2	3	4	5	6	7	8	9	10	11	**12**	**1**	2	3	4	5	**6**
7	**7**	**8**	**9**	**10**	**11**	12	1	2	3	4	5	6	7	8	9	10	11	**12**	**1**	2	3	4	5	**6**
8	**7**	**8**	**9**	**10**	**11**	12	1	2	3	4	5	6	7	8	9	10	11	**12**	**1**	2	3	4	5	**6**
9	**7**	**8**	**9**	**10**	**11**	12	1	2	3	4	5	6	7	8	9	10	11	**12**	**1**	2	3	4	5	**6**
10	**7**	**8**	**9**	**10**	**11**	12	1	2	3	4	5	6	7	8	9	10	11	**12**	**1**	2	3	4	5	**6**
11	**7**	**8**	**9**	**10**	**11**	12	1	2	3	4	5	6	7	8	9	10	11	**12**	**1**	2	3	4	5	**6**
12	**7**	**8**	**9**	**10**	**11**	12	1	2	3	4	5	6	7	8	9	10	11	**12**	**1**	2	3	4	5	**6**
13	**7**	**8**	**9**	**10**	**11**	12	1	2	3	4	5	6	7	8	9	10	11	**12**	**1**	2	3	4	5	**6**
14	**7**	**8**	**9**	**10**	**11**	12	1	2	3	4	5	6	7	8	9	10	11	**12**	**1**	2	3	4	5	**6**
15	**7**	**8**	**9**	**10**	**11**	12	1	2	3	4	5	6	7	8	9	10	11	**12**	**1**	2	3	4	5	**6**
16	**7**	**8**	**9**	**10**	**11**	12	1	2	3	4	5	6	7	8	9	10	11	**12**	**1**	2	3	4	5	**6**
17	**7**	**8**	**9**	**10**	**11**	12	1	2	3	4	5	6	7	8	9	10	11	**12**	**1**	2	3	4	5	**6**
18	**7**	**8**	**9**	**10**	**11**	12	1	2	3	4	5	6	7	8	9	10	11	**12**	**1**	2	3	4	5	**6**
19	**7**	**8**	**9**	**10**	**11**	12	1	2	3	4	5	6	7	8	9	10	11	**12**	**1**	2	3	4	5	**6**
20	**7**	**8**	**9**	**10**	**11**	12	1	2	3	4	5	6	7	8	9	10	11	**12**	**1**	2	3	4	5	**6**
21	**7**	**8**	**9**	**10**	**11**	12	1	2	3	4	5	6	7	8	9	10	11	**12**	**1**	2	3	4	5	**6**
22	**7**	**8**	**9**	**10**	**11**	12	1	2	3	4	5	6	7	8	9	10	11	**12**	**1**	2	3	4	5	**6**
23	**7**	**8**	**9**	**10**	**11**	12	1	2	3	4	5	6	7	8	9	10	11	**12**	**1**	2	3	4	5	**6**
24	**7**	**8**	**9**	**10**	**11**	12	1	2	3	4	5	6	7	8	9	10	11	**12**	**1**	2	3	4	5	**6**
25	**7**	**8**	**9**	**10**	**11**	12	1	2	3	4	5	6	7	8	9	10	11	**12**	**1**	2	3	4	5	**6**
26	**7**	**8**	**9**	**10**	**11**	12	1	2	3	4	5	6	7	8	9	10	11	**12**	**1**	2	3	4	5	**6**
27	**7**	**8**	**9**	**10**	**11**	12	1	2	3	4	5	6	7	8	9	10	11	**12**	**1**	2	3	4	5	**6**
28	**7**	**8**	**9**	**10**	**11**	12	1	2	3	4	5	6	7	8	9	10	11	**12**	**1**	2	3	4	5	**6**
29	**7**	**8**	**9**	**10**	**11**	12	1	2	3	4	5	6	7	8	9	10	11	**12**	**1**	2	3	4	5	**6**
30	**7**	**8**	**9**	**10**	**11**	12	1	2	3	4	5	6	7	8	9	10	11	**12**	**1**	2	3	4	5	**6**
31	**7**	**8**	**9**	**10**	**11**	12	1	2	3	4	5	6	7	8	9	10	11	**12**	**1**	2	3	4	5	**6**

THINGS TO
remember

Mood Tracker

- ◯ Happy
- ◯ Calm
- ◯ Normal
- ◯ Sad
- ◯ Anxious
- ◯ Sick
- ◯ Grumpy
- ◯ Angry
- ◯ Tired
- ◯ Energetic
- ◯
- ◯

SELF-CARE

routine

Body

Mind

It's time to get cozy

Soul

Water Log

COLOUR KEY

:

:

:

:

1
2
3
4
5
6
7
8
9
10
11
12
13
14
15
16
17
18
19
20
21
22
23
24
25
26
27
28
29
30
31

PLAYLIST
december

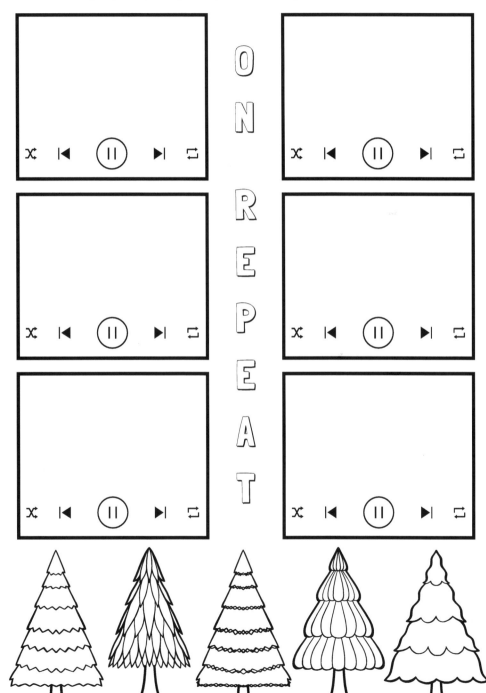

ON REPEAT

Habit Tracker

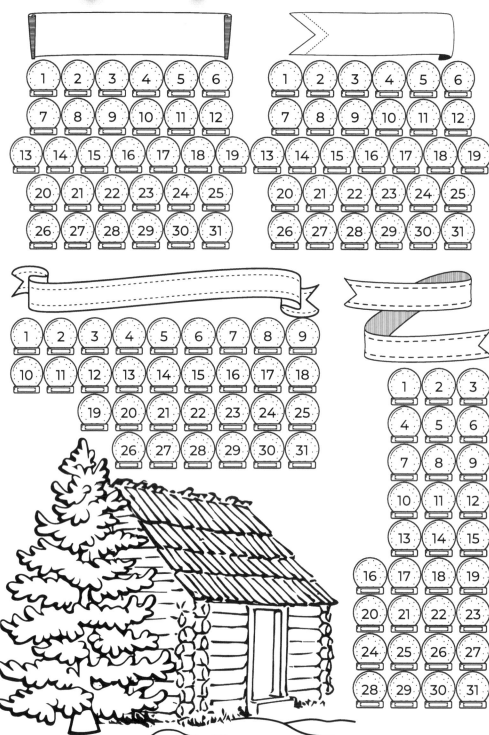

TO-DO LIST
december

NO.	TO DO	Y / N

NOTES

Gratitude Log

1	
2	
3	
4	
5	
6	
7	
8	
9	
10	
11	
12	
13	
14	
15	
16	
17	
18	
19	
20	
21	
22	
23	
24	
25	
26	
27	
28	
29	
30	
31	

VISION
board

MY NOTES

MY DOODLES

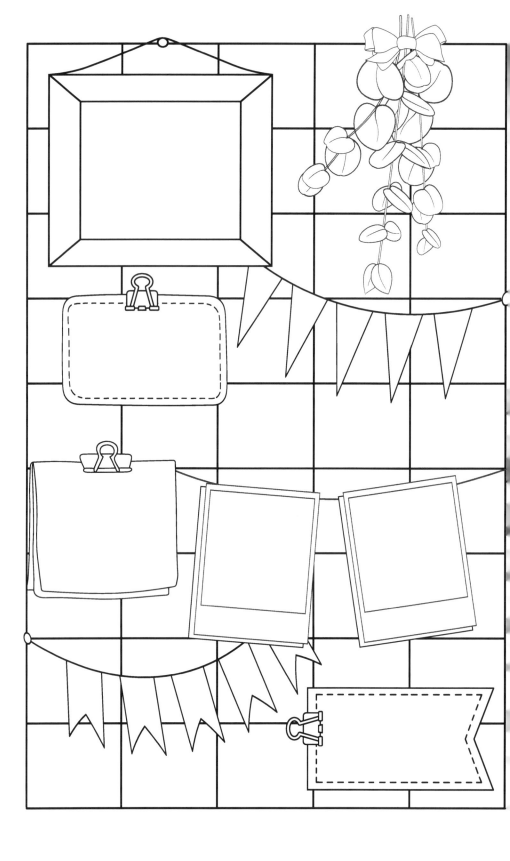

YEARLONG

PAGES

Birthday Log

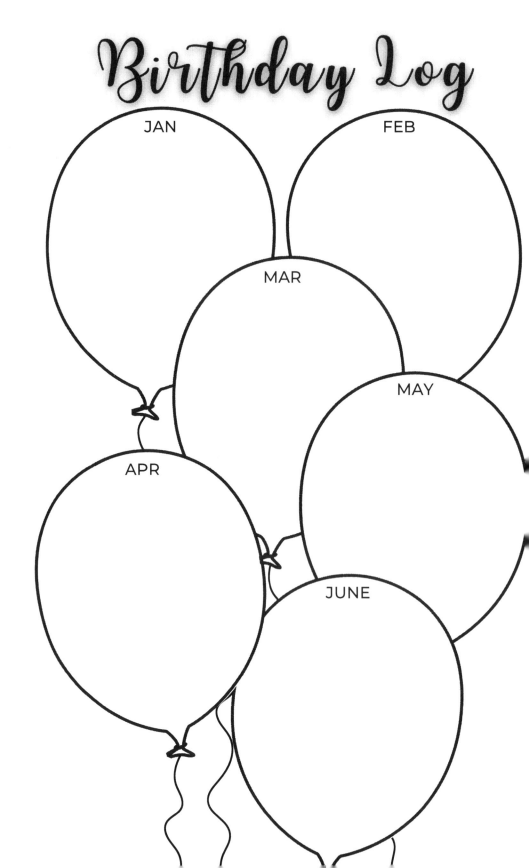

JAN

FEB

MAR

MAY

APR

JUNE

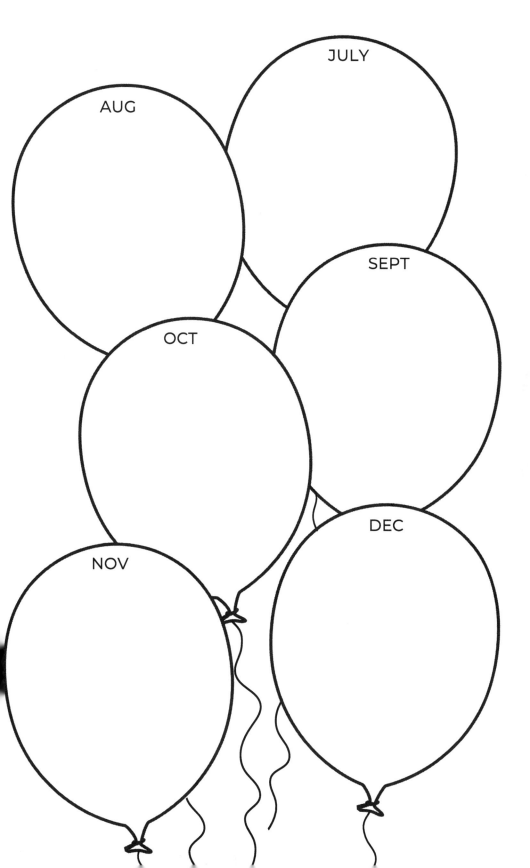

READING
list

Media Tracker

Movie / T.V Show Title	Rating
☰	☆☆☆☆☆
☰	☆☆☆☆☆
☰	☆☆☆☆☆
☰	☆☆☆☆☆
☰	☆☆☆☆☆
☰	☆☆☆☆☆
☰	☆☆☆☆☆
☰	☆☆☆☆☆
☰	☆☆☆☆☆
☰	☆☆☆☆☆
☰	☆☆☆☆☆
☰	☆☆☆☆☆
☰	☆☆☆☆☆
☰	☆☆☆☆☆
☰	☆☆☆☆☆
☰	☆☆☆☆☆

PASSWORD
logbook

Icons		Icons	
☐	User: Pass:	☐	User: Pass:
☐	User: Pass:	☐	User: Pass:
☐	User: Pass:	☐	User: Pass:
☐	User: Pass:	☐	User: Pass:
☐	User: Pass:	☐	User: Pass:
☐	User: Pass:	☐	User: Pass:
☐	User: Pass:	☐	User: Pass:
☐	User: Pass:	☐	User: Pass:

A YEAR IN
pixels

COLOUR KEY

- ☐ :
- ☐ :
- ☐ :
- ☐ :
- ☐ :
- ☐ :

2022

	J	F	M	A	M	J	J	A	S	O	N	D
1												
2												
3												
4												
5												
6												
7												
8												
9												
10												
11												
12												
13												
14												
15												
16												
17												
18												
19												
20												
21												
22												
23												
24												
25												
26												
27												
28												
29												
30												
31												

Manufactured by Amazon.ca
Bolton, ON